INTRODUCTION TO THE GNU/LINUX COMMAND LINE

COMMAND LINE

TABLE OF CONTENTS

INTRODUCTION

1. INTRODUCTION
2. ABOUT THIS MANUAL

1. PUT YOURSELF IN COMMAND

Commands enable you to do all sorts of powerful things on your computer. We'll demonstrate this by looking at an everyday task that might be familiar to you. If you use a digital camera, you probably have a folder full of images on your computer. Imagine you wish to resize the image `profile.jpg` so it is 300 pixels wide and save it as a new image called `profile_small.jpg`.

Using image editing software, the steps you need to go through might look as follows:

1. Open an image editor from the Applications menu.
2. Click the *File>Open* menu item.
3. Browse to the folder with your images.
4. Click the image file `profile.jpg` and then Open.
5. Click the *Image>Scale Image* menu item, for resizing images.
6. Change the image Width to 300 pixels and click *Scale*.
7. Click the *File>Save As* menu item to save the file.
8. Enter `profile_small.jpg` as the new file Name and click *Save*.

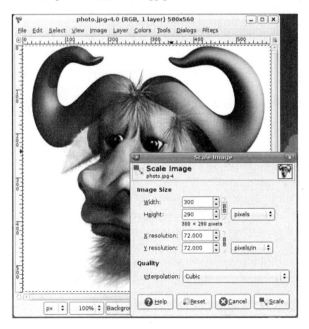

Using the command line, you can achieve the same operation by typing:

```
convert -resize 300 profile.jpg profile_small.jp
```

That's 1 step in the command line instead of 8 steps using the graphical interface. Perhaps you think that the time you spend reading this book and studying the commands isn't worth saving 7 steps. But what if there were 30 images to be resized. Do you still want to open each image individually and repeat the process 30 times using the image editor? That would total 240 steps that you have to go through. Wouldn't you rather just type one command instead and get the job done?

A single command could do the same thing whether you had 30 images, 300 or 3000. This is one of the most compelling reasons to start using the command line. You might start with a slow learning curve, but in the long run, it will save a lot of time. Even more important, learning the command line will open up interesting possibilities and fun ways of working. Let's look at some more reasons why learning the command line is a good idea.

SUMMARIZING THE ADVANTAGES OF USING COMMANDS

Many people who give the command line a try are so amazed by its possibilities that they do not even want to go back to a graphical user interface! Why? Well, in brief, the command line offers the following main advantages over common graphical software:

- **Flexibility.** With graphical programs you sometimes hit a limit, finding that you just can't do what you want or you need to find cumbersome work-arounds to program limits. Working on the command line, though, you can combine commands to yield a virtually infinite range of new and interesting functions. By combining commands creatively, you can make the command line do exactly what you want -- it puts you in control of your computer.
- **Reliability.** Graphical programs are often immature or even unstable. In contrast, most of the tools that the command line offers are highly reliable. One of the reasons for this is their maturity: the oldest command line programs have been around since the late 1970s, which means that they have been tested for three decades. They also tend to work the same way across different operating systems, unlike most graphical tools. If you want a Swiss Army knife you can rely on, the command line is for you.
- **Speed.** Fancy graphics eat up a lot of your hardware's resources, often resulting in slowness or instability. The command line, on the other hand, uses the computer's resources much more sparingly, leaving memory and processing power for the tasks that you actually want to accomplish. The command line is also intrinsically faster: instead of clicking through long chains of graphical menus, you can type commands in a dozen or so keystrokes, and often apply them to multiple files or other objects. If you are a fast typist, this will enable you to drastically increase your productivity.
- **Experience.** Using the command line is a great learning experience. When you use the command line, you communicate with your computer more directly than with graphical programs, thus learning a lot about its inner workings: using the command line on a regular basis is *the* way to becoming a GNU/Linux guru.

- **Fun.** Have you ever wanted to be like those cool computer hackers who can make a
GNU/Linux machine do things that you haven't even dreamed of? Almost all of them do that
using the command line. Once you have learned how to use this powerful tool, you will find
yourself doing fun and interesting stuff that you hadn't even thought to be possible.

THE VALUE OF SCRIPTING

But wait, there's more! You can also store commands in text files. These text files are called
scripts and can be used instead of typing out a long series of commands each time. For example, if
you store commands in a file called `mycommand.sh`, you don't have to type out the commands
again, but simply type :

```
mycommand.sh
```

Additionally you can combine commands together in simple or sophisticated ways. Further, you
can schedule scripts to occur at a specific time or date or at the occurrence of a specific event
on your computer.

You can also write scripts so they accept additional information from you. For example, an image
resizing script might ask you what size the images should be resized to before it starts.

Ever tried to do anything remotely like that by using a Graphical User Interface? Perhaps now
you can see how working with the command line interface starts to open a whole new world to
using your computer.

IS MY COMPUTER SICK?

Another use for the command line is to check the well-being of your computer. There are many
commands you can use to check every facet of your computer's health, from the amount of
space left on the hard drive to the temperature of the CPU. If your computer is acting poorly
and you don't know what the matter is, a few commands will help you quickly determine
whether it's a hardware or software issue, and help you make a quick recovery.

SPANNING THE NETWORK

There is one other interesting feature of command line interfaces that GUIs can't match:
interaction over a network. Imagine you have a computer in another room and you wish to turn
it off. How do you do that? Easy right? Get up, walk to the computer and click on the
"shutdown" button.

Well, those who know how can connect to the computer in the next room via the command
line and type `halt`.

That might seem trivial. Perhaps it's actually better for you to get up off that comfy chair and
expend 5 calories walking to the next room. However, what if the computer you wanted to shut

down was in another suburb? In another city? Another country? Remote control of that computer might then be very useful.

Shutting down a remote computer is just a start. Everything you can do on the command line you can do on the remote computer. That means you can run scripts, execute commands, edit text files, check the diagnostics, and do many other tasks. The world of the command line just got a whole lot bigger.

EVEN GRAPHICAL PROGRAMS ARE COMMANDS

When you click an icon or menu item to start a program, you're running a command. You may find times when it's useful to understand what command you're running. For instance, if you suspect a program is running invisibly in the background and slowing your computer, you can find its command and terminate the program. GUI programs often send more error messages to the CLI, than they show in dialog boxes. This is useful to diagnose problems.

2. ABOUT THIS MANUAL

This manual was initially written at LibrePlanet, the GNU/Linux conference hosted at the Harvard Science Center, Cambridge, MA, on March 21, 22 2009. LibrePlanet was sponsored by the Free Software Foundation (FSF) and organized into three tracks, free software activism, freedom for network services, and high priority free software projects. The creation of this manual was part of the free software activism track, and a collaboration between FLOSS Manuals and the FSF. The book sprint was organized by Andy Oram and Adam Hyde, with assistance from Peter Brown, Deb Nicholson and Danny Clark.

FREE SOFTWARE
F O U N D A T I O N

There was a good turn out for the event. For the first time a FLOSS Manuals book sprint had more authors participating remotely than physically. On the second day of LibrePlanet, and as part of the un-conference schedule, there were 4-5 people working regularly on site.

Big shout out to Tom Boyle for going tip to toe copy editing :)

The FSF has a plan to print and sell two hundred bound copies of this manual at $20 to provide funds for the second Gnubie book sprint. You can purchase this book for that purpose at:

http://shop.fsf.org/product/Introduction_to_Command_Line/

This manual has been written within FLOSS Manuals. This manual can be improved by you. To improve this manual follow these steps:

1. REGISTER

Register at FLOSS Manuals:
http://en.flossmanuals.net/register

2. CONTRIBUTE!

Select the manual (http://en.flossmanuals.net/bin/view/CommandLineIntro) and a chapter to work on.

If you need to ask us questions about how to contribute then join the chat room listed below and ask us! We look forward to your contribution!

For more information on using FLOSS Manuals you may also wish to read our manual:
http://en.flossmanuals.net/FLOSSManuals

You may wish to also look at the Outline at the end of the book. This is a guide as to how the manual might be extended. Feel free to change the outline and improvise!

http://en.flossmanuals.net/bin/view/CommandLineIntro/Outline

3. CHAT

It's a good idea to talk with us so we can help co-ordinate all contributions. We have a chat room embedded in the FLOSS Manuals website so you can use it in the browser.

If you know how to use IRC you can connect to the following:
server: irc.freenode.net
channel: #flossmanuals

4. MAILING LIST

For discussing all things about FLOSS Manuals join our mailing list:
http://lists.flossmanuals.net/listinfo.cgi/discuss-flossmanuals.net

5. TRANSLATION

If you would like to translate this manual then let us know as we have a very good system to enable translations. To start a translation join the mailing list (listed above) and send an email telling us which language you would like to translate the manual into.

BASICS

3. GETTING STARTED
4. BEGINNING SYNTAX
5. MOVING AROUND
6. FILE STRUCTURE

3. GETTING STARTED

Modern computing is highly interactive, and using the command line is just another form of interaction. Most people use the computer through its desktop or graphical interface, interacting at a rapid pace. They click on an object, drag and drop it, double-click another to open it, alter it, etc.

Although interactions happen so fast you don't think about it, each click or keystroke is a command to the computer, which it reacts to. Using the command line is the same thing, but more deliberate. You type a command and press the **Return** or **Enter** key. For instance, in my terminal I type:

```
date
```

And the computer replies with:

```
Thu Mar 12 17:15:09 EDT 2009
```

That's pretty computerish. In later chapters we'll explain how to request the date and time in a more congenial format. We'll also explain how working in different countries and with different languages changes the output. The idea is that you've just had an interaction.

THE COMMAND LINE CAN DO MUCH BETTER

The *date* command, as seen so far, compares poorly with the alternative of glancing at a calendar or clock. The main problem is not the unappetizing appearance of the output, mentioned already, but the inability to do anything of value with the output. For instance, if I'm looking at the date in order to insert it into a document I'm writing or update an event on my online calendar, I have to do some retyping. The command line can do much better.

After you learn basic commands and some nifty ways to save yourself time, you'll find out more in this book about feeding the output of commands into other commands, automating activities, and saving commands for later use.

WHAT DO WE MEAN BY A COMMAND?

At the beginning of this chapter we used the word "command" very generally to refer to any way of telling the computer what to do. But in the context of this book, a command has a very specific meaning. It's a file on your computer that can be executed. Except for a few commands that are executed directly (called *built-in commands*), the computer runs each command by finding the file that bears its name and executing that file. We'll give you more details as they become useful.

WAYS TO ENTER COMMANDS

To follow along on this book, you need to open a command-line interpreter (called a *shell* or *terminal* in GNU/Linux) on your computer. Pre-graphical computer screens used to present people with this interpreter as soon as they logged in. Nowadays almost everybody except professional system administrators uses a graphical interface. So we'll show you how to pull up a shell.

FINDING A TERMINAL

Virtually every desktop interface provides a program that mimics the old text-only terminals that computers used to offer as interfaces. On your desktop, try looking through the menus of applications for a program called Terminal. Often it's on a menu named something such as "Accessories", which is not really fair because once you read this book you'll be spending a lot of time in the terminal every day.

In GNOME you choose **Applications -> Accessories -> Terminal**

Wherever it's located, you can almost certainly find a terminal program.

When you run the terminal program, it just shows a blank window; there's not much in the way of help. You're expected to know what to do--and we'll show you.

The following figure shows the Terminal window opened on the desktop in GNOME.

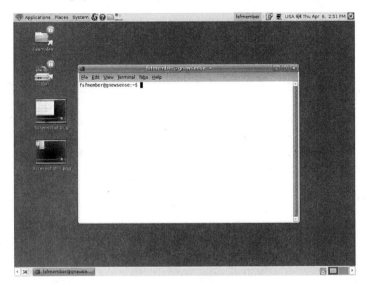

RUNNING AN INDIVIDUAL COMMAND

Many graphical interfaces also provide a small dialog box called something like "Run command". It presents a small text area where you can type in a command and press the Return or Enter key.

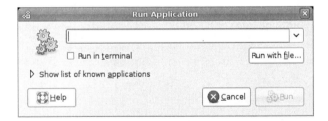

You can use this box as a shortcut to quickly start up a terminal program, as long as you know the name of a terminal program installed on your computer. If you are working on an unfamiliar computer and don't even know the name of the default terminal program, try typing "xterm" to start up a no-frills terminal program (no fancy menus allowing choice of color themes or fonts).

HOW WE SHOW COMMANDS AND OUTPUT IN THIS BOOK

There's a common convention in books about the command-line. When you start up a terminal, you see a little string (a string is a sequence of characters like "almond" or "eiessj44ik" or "almond34") indicating that the terminal is ready to accept your command. This string is called a *prompt*, and it may be as simple as:

$

After you type your command and press the **Return** or **Enter** key, the terminal displays the command's output (if there is any) followed by another prompt. So my earlier interaction would be shown in the book like this:

```
$ date
Thu Mar 12 17:15:09 EDT 2009
$
```

You have to know how to interpret examples like the preceding one. All you type here is *date*. Then press the **Return** key. The word *date* in the example is printed in bold to indicate that it's something you type. The rest is output on the terminal.

4. THE PARTS OF A COMMAND

The first word you type on a line is the command you wish to run. In the "Getting Started" section we saw a call to the `date` command, which returned the current date and time.

ARGUMENTS

Another command we could use is `echo`, which displays the specified information back to the user. This isn't very useful if we don't actually specify information to display. Fortunately, we can add more information to a command to modify its behavior; this information consists of *arguments* . Luckily, the `echo` command doesn't argue back; it just repeats what we ask it:

```
$ echo foo
foo
```

In this case, the argument was **foo**, but there is no need to limit the number of arguments to one. Every word of the text entered, excluding the first word, will be considered an additional argument passed to the command. If we wanted `echo` to respond with multiple words, such as **foo bar**, we could give it multiple arguments:

```
$ echo foo bar
foo bar
```

Arguments are normally separated by "white space" (blanks and tabs -- things that show up white on paper). It doesn't matter how many spaces you type, so long as there is at least one. For instance, if you type:

```
$ echo foo            bar
foo bar
```

with a lot of spaces between the two arguments, the "extra" spaces are ignored, and the output shows the two arguments separated by a single space.

OPTIONS

Revisiting the date command, suppose you actually wanted the UTC date/time information displayed. For this, date provides the --utc option. Notice the two initial hyphens. These indicate arguments that a command checks when it starts and that control its behavior. The date command checks specially for the --utc option and says, "OK, I know you're asking for UTC time." This is different from arguments we invented, as when we issued echo with the arguments foo bar.

Other than the dashes preceding the word, --utc is entered just like an argument:

```
$ date --utc
Tue Mar 24 18:12:44 UTC 2009
```

Usually, you can shorten these options to a shorter value such as **date -u** (the shorter version often has only one hyphen). Short options are quicker to type (use them when you are typing at the shell), whereas long options are easier to read (use them in scripts).

Now let's say we wanted to look at yesterday's date instead of today's. For this we would want to specify the --date argument, which takes an argument of its own. The argument for an option is simply the word following that option. In this case, the command would be date --date yesterday.

Since options are just arguments, you can combine options together to create more sophisticated behaviour. For instance, we could combined the previous two options to get the UTC information from yesterday you would type:

```
$ date --date yesterday -u
Mon Mar 23 18:16:58 UTC 2009
```

REPEATING COMMANDS

Use the up arrow key to retrieve a command you issued before. You can move up and down using arrow keys to get earlier and later commands. The left arrow and right arrow keys let you move around inside a single command. Combined with the **Backspace** key, these let you change parts of the command and turn it into a new one. Each time you press the **Enter** key, you submit the command to the terminal and it runs.

5. MOVING AROUND

Anyone who has used a graphical interface has moved between folders. A typical view of folders appears in Figure 1, where someone has opened a home directory, then a folder named "my-stuff" under that, and a folder named "music" under that.

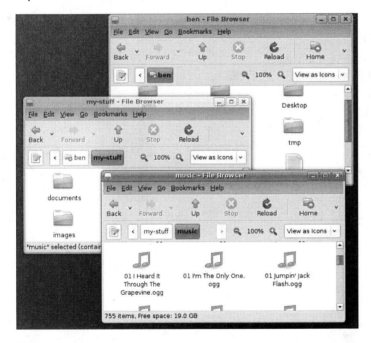

Figure 1 : Folders

When you use the command line, folders are called directories. That's just an older term used commonly in computing to refer to collections of things. Anything you do in a folder on the desktop is reflected in the directory when you're on the command line, and vice versa. The desktop and the command line are just two ways of viewing the same directory/folder, namely */home/username/Desktop/* (where username is your username, e.g. if you are called "joe" it would be */home/joe/Desktop/*).

Files contain your information--whether pictures, text, music, spreadsheet data, or something else--while the directories are containers for files. Directories can also store other directories.

You'll be much more comfortable with the command line once you can move around directories, view them, create and remove them, and so on.

Directories are organized, in turn, into filesystems. Your hard disk has one type of filesystem, a CD-ROM or DVD has another, a USB mass storage device has yet another, and so on. That's why a CD-ROM, DVD, or USB device shows up as something special on the desktop when you insert it. Luckily, you don't have to worry much about the differences because both the desktop and the terminal can hide the differences. But sometimes in this book we'll talk about the information a filesystem has about your files.

The "first" directory is called the root and is represented by the name / (just a forward slash). You can think of all the directories and files on the system as a tree that grows upside-down from this root (Figure 2):

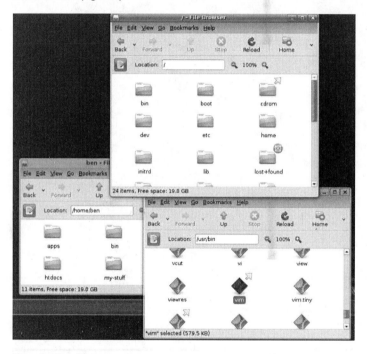

Figure 2 : Root Directory

ABSOLUTE AND RELATIVE PATHS

Every file and directory in the system has an "address" called its absolute path or sometimes just its path. It describes the route you have to follow starting from the root that would take you to that particular file or directory.

For example, suppose you like the vim editor that we'll introduce in a later chapter, and are told you can start it by running the command `/usr/bin/vim`. This point underlines what we said in an earlier chapter: commands are just executable files. So the vim editor is a file with the path *lusrlbinlvim*, and if you run that command `/usr/bin/vim` you will execute the editor. As you can see from these examples, the slash / is also used as a separator between directories.

Can you find *lusrlbinlvim* in Figure 2? The pathname can be interpreted as follows:

1. Start at the root (/) directory.
2. Move from / down to a directory named *usr*.
1. Move from *usr* down to a directory named *bin*.
2. *vim* is located in that directory.

You are just getting used to the command line, and it may feel odd to be typing while reading this book. If you feel any confusion in this section, try scribbling the directory tree in Figure 2 on paper. Draw arrows on the paper as you run the commands in this section, to help orient you to where you are.

Note that you can't tell whether something is a file or a directory just by looking at its path.

When you work with the command line you will be always working "in" a directory. You can find the path of this directory using the command `pwd` (print working directory), like this:

```
$ pwd
/home/ben
```

You can see that `pwd` prints an absolute path. If you want to switch your working directory you can use the command `cd` (change directory) followed by an argument which points to the target directory:

```
$ cd /
```

You just changed your working directory to the root of the filesystem! If you want to return to the previous directory, you can enter the command:

```
$ cd /home/ben
```

As an alternative, you can "work your way" back to *lhomelben* using relative paths. They are called that because they are specified "in relation" to your current working directory. If you go back to the root directory, you could enter the following commands:

```
$ cd /
$ cd home
$ cd ben
$ pwd
/home/ben
```

The first command changes your current working directory to the root. The second changes to *home*, relative to /, making your current working directory */home*. The third command changes it to *ben*, relative to */home*, landing you in */home/ben*.

Good to be back home

Every user in the system has a directory assigned to him or her, called the home directory. No matter what your current working directory is, you can quickly return to your home directory like this:

```
$ cd
```

That is, enter the `cd` command without any arguments.

All your files and preferences are stored in your home directory (or its subdirectories). Every user of your system with a login account gets her own home directory. Home directories are named the same as users' login names, and are usually found in */home*, although a few systems have them in */usr/home*. When you start your terminal, it will place you in your home directory.

There's a special shortcut to refer to your home directory, namely the symbol ~ (usually called a tilde, and found near the very left top of most keyboards). You can use it as part of more complex path expressions, and it will always refer to your home directory. For example, *~/Desktop* refers to the directory called *Desktop* that usually exists within your home directory.

The . and .. directories

The entries . and .. are special and they exist in every directory, even /. The parent of root, */..*, is root itself. The first one is a shorthand for "this directory." You can use it as a relative path, and you can try and see what happens when you do this:

```
$ pwd
/usr/bin
$ cd .
$ pwd
/usr/bin
```

If *vim* is in */usr/bin*, at this point you could run it by typing the relative path:

```
$ ./vim
```

The second special directory, "..", is a shorthand for "the parent directory of this directory." Continuing from the previous example, you can do this:

```
$ cd ..
$ pwd
/usr
```

Since they are actual entries in the filesystem, you can use them as part of more complex paths, for example:

```
$ cd /usr/bin
$ pwd
/usr/bin
$ cd ../lib
$ pwd
/usr/lib
$ cd ../..
$ pwd
/
$ cd home
$ pwd
/home
$ cd ../usr/bin
$ pwd
/usr/bin
```

Try moving around your computer on the command line and you will soon get used to it!

6. FILES AND DIRECTORIES

Although you're most interested in files in your own folder or directory, it helps to know what else is on your system. In this chapter we'll look around a GNU/Linux system.

Here is a list of the most common directories right beneath the root directory (the one whose name is just "/"):

```
/bin      basic programs (Programs that are absolutely needed,
          shell and commands only)
/boot     initialization files (Required to actually boot your computer)
/dev      device files (Describe physical stuff like hard disks
          and partitions)
/etc      configuration files
/home     users' home directories
/lib      basic libraries (Required by the basic programs)
/media    mount points for removable media
/mnt      mount points (For system admins who need to temporarily
          mount a filesystem)
/opt      third-party programs
/proc     proc filesystem (Describe processes and status info,
          not stored on disk)
/root     system administrator's files
/sbin     basic administration programs (Like bin, but only
          usable by administators)
/srv      service-specific files
/sys      sys filesystem (Similar to proc, stored in memory
          based filesytem: tempfs)
/tmp      temporary files (Files not kept between boots, often in tempfs)
/usr      users' programs (Another bin, lib, sbin, plus local,
          share, src, and more)
/var      variable data preserved between reboots
```

You don't need to know about the directory structure outside your home directory in order to run applications, but this knowledge occasionally comes in handy. Perhaps the most common uses are when you want to change a system-wide configuration file or view log messages. Log files generally contain progress information and error reports from programs, and may reveal the source of problems (bugs, configuration errors, missing or corrupted files) on your system. Many log files are kept in the /var/log directory, but some programs put their log files in hidden directories in the user's home directory. An example is ~/.sugar/default/logs.

Historically, GNU/Linux system configuration was done through editing text files. Today, most popular GNU/Linux systems encourage users to make changes to the system configuration through graphical administration tools. Sometimes however, this is not possible or desirable, and you may find yourself editing the configuration files in a text editor. This is usually trickier, as you need to know where these files are and how to edit them, and in some cases you also need to signal or restart a running program so it will read in your changes. That said, this method has its advantages, such as the ability to configure computers with no graphics capabilities, or configure programs that have no graphical configuration program.

COMMANDS

7. BASIC COMMANDS
8. CUT DOWN ON TYPING
9. SUPERUSERS
10. REDIRECTION

7. BASIC COMMANDS

By now you have some basic knowledge about directories and files and you can interact with the command line interface. We can learn some of the commands you'll be using many times each day.

ls

The first thing you likely need to know before you can start creating and making changes to files is *what's already there?* With a graphical interface you'd do this by opening a folder and inspecting its contents. From the command line you use the program `ls` instead to list a folder's contents.

```
$ ls
Desktop   Documents   Music   Photos
```

By default, `ls` will use a very compact output format. Many terminals show the files and subdirectories in different colors that represent different file types. Regular files don't have special coloring applied to their names. Some file types, like JPEG or PNG images, or tar and ZIP files, are usually colored differently, and the same is true for programs that you can run and for directories. Try `ls` for yourself and compare the icons and emblems your graphical file manager uses with the colors that ls applies on the command line. If the output isn't colored, you can call `ls` with the option `--color`:

```
$ ls --color
```

man & apropos

You can learn about options and arguments using another program called `man` (man is short for manual) like this:

```
$ man ls
```

Here, `man` is being asked to bring up the manual page for `ls`. You can use the arrow keys to scroll up and down in the screen that appears and you can close it using the **q** key (for quit).

You can also use `man` to learn about new programs. Let's say you want to rename files using the command line but you don't know the name of the program that you can use for that. You can use another program called `apropos` for that, like this:

```
$ apropos rename
...
mv (1)                    - move (rename) files
prename (1)               - renames multiple files
rename (2)                - change the name or location of a file
...
```

Here, `apropos` searches the manual pages that `man` knows about and prints commands it thinks are related to renaming. On your computer this command might (and probably will) display more information but it's very likely to include the entries shown.

Note how the program names include a number besides them. That number is called their *section*, and most programs that you can use from the command line will be in section 1. You can pass `apropos` an option to display results from section 1 manuals only, like this:

```
$ apropos -s 1 rename
...
mv (1)                    - move (rename) files
prename (1)               - renames multiple files
...
```

At this stage, the section number isn't terribly important. Just know that section 1 manual pages are the ones that apply to programs you use on the command line. To see a list of the other sections, look up the manual page for man using `man man`.

mv

Looking at the results from `apropos`, that `mv` program looks interesting. You can use it like this:

```
$ mv oldname newname
```

Just as the description provided by `apropos` suggests, this program moves files. If the last argument happens to be an *existing* directory, `mv` will move the file to that directory instead of renaming it. Because of this, you can provide `mv` more than two arguments:

```
$ mv one_file another_file a_third_file ~/stuff
```

If ~/*stuff* exists, then `mv` will move the files there. If it doesn't exist, it will produce an error message, like this:

```
$ mv one_file another_file a_third_file stuff
mv: target 'stuff' is not a directory
```

mkdir

How do you create a directory, anyway? Use the mkdir command:

```
$ mkdir ~/stuff
```

And how do you remove it? With the rmdir command:

```
$ rmdir ~/stuff
```

If the directory you wish to remove is not empty, rmdir will produce an error message and will not remove it. If you want to remove a directory that contains files, you have to empty it first. To see how this is done, we will need to create a directory and put some files in it first. These files we can remove safely later. Let's start by creating a directory called *practice* in your home and change the current working directory there:

```
$ mkdir ~/practice
$ cd ~/practice
```

cp, rm & rmdir

Now let's copy some files there using the program cp. We are going to use some files that are very likely to exist on your computer, so the following commands should work for you:

```
$ cp /etc/fstab /etc/hosts /etc/issue /etc/motd .
$ ls
fstab  hosts  issue  motd
```

Don't forget the dot at the end of the line! Remember it means "this directory". As you can see, you have to give cp a list of files you wish to copy and a destination. Now, if you go back to your home and try to remove the directory called *practice*, rmdir will produce an error message:

```
$ cd ..
$ rmdir practice
rmdir: failed to remove 'practice': Directory not empty
```

You can use the program rm to remove the files first, like this:

```
$ rm practice/fstab practice/hosts practice/issue practice/motd
```

And now you can try removing the directory again:

```
$ rmdir practice
```

And now it works, without showing any output.

But what happens if your directories have directories inside that also have files, you could be there for weeks making sure each folder is empty! The `rm` command solves this problem through an option called −r, which stands for "recursive." In the following example, the command fails because *foo* is not a plain file:

```
$ rm foo/
rm: cannot remove `foo/`: Is a directory
```

So maybe you try `rmdir`, but that fails because *foo* has something else under it:

```
$ rmdir foo
rmdir: foo: File exists
```

So you use `rm −r`, which succeeds and does not produce a message.

```
$ rm -r foo/
```

So when you have a big directory, you don't have to go and empty every subdirectory.

But be warned that −r is a very powerful argument and you may lose data you wanted to keep!

cat & less

You don't need an editor to view the contents of a file. What you need is just to display it. The `cat` program fits the bill here:

```
$ cat myspeech.txt
Friends, Romans, Countrymen! Lend me your ears!
```

Here, `cat` just opens the file *myspeech.txt* and prints the entire file to your screen, as fast as it can. However if the file is really long, the contents will go by very quickly, and when `cat` is done, all you will see are the last few lines of the file. To just view the contents of a long file (or any text file) you can use the `less` program:

```
$ less myspeech.txt
```

Just as with using `man`, use the arrow keys to navigate, and press **q** to quit.

COMMAND LINE

8. ALL THAT TYPING...

So, all this typing has got to stop being fun at some point. Fortunately, the command line offers a number of ways to make your work more efficient.

AUTO COMPLETION

Every keyboard has a **Tab** key, and its a very useful thing to have in the terminal. You might have used this keystroke before to indent words in a word processor. You can still do this in GNU/Linux word processors, but when you use **Tab** in the GNU/Linux terminal it becomes such a time saver that when you master it you will be using it all the time.

Essentially, the **Tab** is an auto-complete command. If, for example, I want to move the file 'dsjkdshdsdsjhds_ddsjw22.txt' somewhere with the mv command I can either type out every letter of the stupid filename, or I can type mv (for 'move') followed by the first few letters of the filename and press **Tab**. The rest of the filename will be automagically filled in. If the filename is not filled in it means that there are several files (or directories) that start with those first few letters I typed. To remedy this I could type a few more letters of the filename and press **Tab** again, or to help me out I could press **Tab** twice and it will give me a list of files that start with those letters.

You can also use **Tab** to auto-complete command names.

Tab is your friend, use it a lot.

COPY AND PASTE

Just because you are working on the command line doesn't mean you can't use some of the conveniences you are used to in the GUI. While cut and paste may work a little differently here from its behavior in other operating systems, you'll soon find it very intuitive.

Copying text is as simple as highlighting the text you wish to copy by holding down the left mouse button and highlighting the text as you are probably already used to doing.

Pasting text The highlighted text that you just copied is held in the clipboard until you paste it where your cursor is by clicking the middle (wheel) mouse button.

Try it! Select the paragraph below with the left mouse button, open a new virtual terminal, and paste the text with the middle mouse button.

```
echo "This is pasted text."
```

After you see the text in the terminal, press the **Enter** key and the `echo` command will repeat the text between the quotes on the command line.

Note : If you are copying text from a web page, sometimes the punctuation isn't handled properly. You might actually copy some unseen formatting along with the text, which will break the syntax of the command you are copying.

HISTORY

It is also possible to use the up and down arrows on the keyboard to navigate back and forwards through the history of the commands you have typed. When you navigate to an earlier command this way, it is then just necessary to press the **Return** or **Enter** key and the command will be re-executed.

9. THE SUPERUSER (ROOT)

Some parts of the computer system are thought to require special protection. If somebody can change the basic `cat` or `less` command, for instance, they could cause you to corrupt your own files. So certain commands must be run only by special privileges called *superuser* or *root* privileges.

In the days when computer systems cost hundreds of thousands of dollars and were shared by hundreds of people, *root* was assigned to an actual person (or a small group) who constituted a kind of priesthood. Nowadays every owner of a PC can execute superuser commands (this is not always true on mobile devices, though). There is still a user account on each GNU/Linux system called *root*. This allows the system to make this user the owner of sensitive system files.

The *root* user, incidentally, has nothing to do with the root directory (the / directory) in the filesystem.

Superuser commands are powerful and must be used carefully, but their use is quite common. For instance, whenever a desktop user installs software, he or she must become superuser for a few minutes.

THE SUDO COMMAND

On many modern systems, whenever you want to enter a superuser command, you just precede it with `sudo`:

```
$ sudo rm -r /junk_directory
```

You are then prompted for your password, so nobody walking up casually to your system could execute a dangerous command. The system keeps your password around for a while, so you can enter further superuser commands without the bother of re-entering the password.

Systems also provide a `su` command that logs you in as superuser and gives you a new shell prompt. Not all systems allow users to use it, though, because you can get carried away, start doing everyday work as superuser --and suddenly realize you've trashed your system through a typo. It is much safer to do your home system administration using `sudo`.

If other people share your system and you want to give someone superuser privileges, for this you need to know a little more about System Administration.

10. REDIRECTION

Output redirection is one of the very powerful, and easily misunderstood, parts of the shell. To decrease misunderstandings, we'll keep to the basics.

The > operator (an "operator" is a symbol like +,-,<,> that represents a specific action) is for redirecting output. In a very simple example, if you want to list the files in a directory, you type `ls`. That output goes to your screen. If you want that list instead to go to a file, however, you'd do something like this:

```
$ ls > my-file-list
```

The file *my-file-list* now contains all of the files in your directory. (If you ran the same command again, you'd also get the file *my-file-list* in your list.)

The > operator is a "clobbering" operator -- if you are outputting to an existing file, it will overwrite the old contents. Sometimes, especially if you are keeping a logfile, what you want is the >> operator. It works the same way as the > operator, except that it appends to the end of an existing file. (If the file doesn't yet exist, it creates it.)

There are other places you can redirect output to, like device special files such as terminals, or */dev/null*, which is an infinitely big empty bucket (or more accurately it just ignores all input). If you have a program that you know will produce voluminous output you don't care about, you could do this:

```
$ bigprogram > /dev/null
```

The program will execute normally, but you won't see its normal output. (You would, however, see any of its error output; more detail below under File Descriptors).

The < operator is for redirecting input. Most programs that would expect input from your terminal are happy to accept it from another source instead, such as an existing file.

For example, if you wish to email the contents of *myfile.txt* to joe you could do this:

```
$ mail joe < myfile.txt
```

The redirection operators are particularly relevant for jobs running in the background. If you run a non-graphical program in the background, it just runs quietly unless it produces output. Any output it produces goes to your terminal as usual, so you may want to avoid confusion by redirecting output to a file. For instance, the following places the output from `sort` into *big_file_sorted* and any error messages into *big_file_err*. This way, no output can confuse you by appearing at the terminal:

```
$ sort big_file >big_file_sorted 2>big_file_err &
```

A program running in the background cannot accept input from the terminal. So if you mistakenly put such a program in the background (and don't redirect input from a file through the < operator), it will get stuck waiting when it has to accept input.

ADVANCED-ISH

11. CHEAPER BY THE DOZEN

After getting used to the command line, you will start looking for ways to do more in less time. One of the easiest ways to achieve that is to work on multiple files at the same time, so that instead of:

```
$ rm this
$ rm that
$ rm here
$ rm there
```

you just remove all those files with one command. Many commands, including rm, let you simply specify all the files you want to delete as arguments in one go:

```
$ rm this that here there
```

Still, there has to be a better way!

GLOBBING

File globbing is the shell's way of dealing with multiple files with the fewest characters possible. The shell treats certain characters as codes that you can use to specify groups of things you want the commands to affect. These characters are commonly called "wildcards" because they're like a card in a game that the players have designated to represent anything you want.

The "*" Wildcard

Imagine a directory of files:

```
$ ls
here    that    there   this
```

that you want to delete. A tedious job can be turned simple by using the * or asterisk wildcard.

```
$ rm *
```

When used by itself, the asterisk wildcard refers to all the files in the directory. We say that the shell *expands* the wildcard. Knowing what's in the directory, the shell substitutes those filenames for the asterisk and effectively executes the following command:

```
$ rm here that there this
```

You can combine * with other characters, however, to make it selective.

```
$ rm t*
$ ls
here
```

What happened here? The shell looked at "t" first and then expanded the asterisk to cover all the files that begin with "t". If you had requested "h*" instead, the shell would have removed any file that started with an "h". Let's restore the original files and see what happens:

```
$ rm h*
$ ls
that    there   this
```

The asterisk wildcard can be placed anywhere within a word. Let's switch to an `ls` command because it's easier to see what's happening with wildcards:

```
$ ls th*re
there
```

By switching from `rm` to `ls` we see an important aspect of wildcard: you can use them with any command, because the shell interprets them before it even invokes the command. In fact, you can't issue a command *without* taking into account the behavior of wildcards, because they're a feature of the shell. (Luckily, you're not likely to ever have to deal with a filename that contains a real asterisk.)

Multiple asterisks can also be used together. For instance, in this way you can find filenames where the middle of a series is the same, but they start and end differently. Let's try it on the original four files:

```
$ ls *i*
this
```

People often use the asterisk to remove files that are all of one type. For instance, if you've been working with a lot of photos and want to clean up files ending in *.jpg* when you're finished, you can remove all the ones in the current directly as follows:

```
$ rm *.jpg
```

Suppose you have some files ending in *.jpg* and some ending in *.jpeg*. The asterisk still makes clean-up easy:

```
$ ls *.jp*g
```

And suppose the JPEG files are scattered among several subdirectories. You have directories named photos1, photos2, photos3, and so forth, each containing JPEGs you want to remove. A wildcard can help you list all the contents of those subdirectories:

```
$ ls photos*
photos1:
centraal_station.jpg      nieuwe_kerk.jpg

photos2:
ica.jpeg                  sanders_theater.jpeg

photos3:
bayeux_cathedral.jpeg    rouen_cathedral.jpeg      travel.odt
```

And you can specify a directory along with the filenames you remove:

```
$ rm photos*/*.jp*g
$ ls photos*
photos1:

photos2:

photos3:
travel.odt
```

Only the *travel.odt* file remains (because it doesn't match ".jp*g") as a record of all the trips you've taken.

There is, however, one limit to the asterisk wildcard. By default, it will not match any hidden files (those with filenames that start with a dot, you need to `ls -a` to see these).

```
$ ls -a
.

..

.hidden
this
that
here
there
$ rm *
$ ls -a
.

..

.hidden
```

If you want those hidden files deleted by a wildcard it is necessary to append a dot to the front of the wildcard. Note that normal files (those that are not hidden/do not start with a dot) will not be deleted when you do this:

```
$ ls -a
.

..

.hidden
here
$ rm .*
$ ls -a
.

..

here
```

Finally, it's important to note that the asterisk can also match when nothing is there. In the following listing, *task* is listed along with files that have something to match the asterisk:

```
$ ls task*
task   taskA   taskB   taskXY
```

The "?" Wildcard

The "?" or question mark wildcard is very similar to the asterisk wildcard. The crucial difference is that the question mark wildcard takes the place of only one character.

```
$ ls task*
task   taskA   taskB   taskXY
$ ls task?
taskA   taskB
$ ls task??
taskXY
```

As we've already seen, the asterisk matches all the files beginning with "task". A single question mark matches files that have a single character after "task". The double question mark requires exactly two characters in that position.

The "[ ]" Wildcards

The square brackets wildcards can get even more specific, denoting a ranges of characters. The following ls command includes a −1 (the digit "one") option, which means "list one entry on each line." This makes it easier to see how the files in this example differ.

```
$ ls -1
file_1
file_2
file_3
file_a
file_b
file_c
```

By using the square brackets, you can remove specific files without typing every name completely.

```
$ rm file_[1,3,a,c]
$ ls -1
file_2
file_b
```

You can also specify a bunch of individual characters without the commas (they are optional). You could get the same effect through:

```
$ rm file_[13ac]
```

Furthermore, within the square brackets, the order of the characters doesn't matter.

Combining square brackets with a hyphen, you can also do ranges of files. Let's start with a directory containing lots of files ending in numbers:

```
$ ls
file_1
file_2
file_3
...
file_9
```

At first it might be tempting to use the asterisk wildcard here. However, what if we need to remove only files 2-6? We could use the comma-separated form of the square brackets wildcard, but you would still have to type five numbers, plus the commas. Fortunately, there is a much easier way.

```
$ rm file_[2-6]
```

Now the only files left are files 1 and 7-9. By using the dash between a set of numerals in the square brackets, you make the shell expand the pattern by creating a name with every number between the starting value to the left of the dash and the end value to the right.

Ranges aren't just for numbers. They can also use letters.

```
$ ls -1
file_a
file_b
file_c
file_d
$ rm file_[a-c]
$ ls -1
file_d
```

Both commas and ranges can be combined into the same instance of square brackets.

```
$ ls -1
file_a
file_b
file_c
file_1
file_2
$ rm file_[a-c,1,2]
$ ls
```

BRACE EXPANSION

We've seen the ability to get a range of characters or letters that fall in a single digit range (0-9 in our examples) but what about when you need to match a range of files that uses double or even triple digits?

```
$ ls -1
file_1
file_2
file_3
...
file_78
$ rm file_[1-20]
$ ls -1
file_3
...
file_78
```

Since the brackets glob can only interpret single character ranges it interrupts, "1-20" not as a range but as the characters: "1", "-", "2", and "0". Causing only "file_1" and "file_2" to be deleted because the are the only ones that match. If you want to access ranges larger than 0-9, you have to using Bash's brace expansion, "{start..end}".

```
$ rm file_{1..20}
```

In a brace range the double dot is the delimiter instead of a dash.

Braces can also be used when you need to get a series of files that have a common pattern but subtle differences. Such as with:

```
$ ls
file.txt
file.pdf
file.pl
file.odf
```

If you just wanted to delete the *pdf*, *odf*, and *txt* files you could specify a comma separated list of strings in a brace pair:

```
$ rm file.{txt,pdf,odf}
$ ls
file.pl
```

GLOBBING WHEN NO FILE MATCHES

Suppose you specify a wildcard and the shell can't find any matching filename:

```
$ ls -1
file_a
file_b
file_c
file_d
$ rm file?
rm: cannot remove `file?': No such file or directory
```

When there is no file to match a pattern, the shell passes the wildcard to the program unexpanded. That's why you get an error message from the `rm` program, not from the shell.

DISABLING A WILDCARD

Okay, we know the shell will pass a wildcard as an option to a program when it can't find a file, but what do we do when we want to send a character that also happens to be a wildcard to our program? Here's a common example: we want to search a file for every occurrence of an asterisk.

```
$ ls
2file
*file
*?****[a-b]
```

Now we happen to want *file, but we get:

```
*file    2file
```

Why? Because the asterisk is a wildcard, the shell expanded it before sending it to `ls`. So after expansion, the command would look like:

```
$ ls *file 2file
```

If we want `ls` to find an asterisk something different is in order.

The "\", or backslash, tells the shell to treat the following character as a normal character and do no expansion.

```
$ ls \*file
*file
```

Because the asterisk is the next character after the backslash, the shell sends the asterisk to `ls` unmodified. In other words: the backslash *escapes* the asterisk.

The backslash modifier works well when we have only one wildcard character that we want to pass to a program, but what if we wanted to pass a string like ***?****[a-b]** with lots of characters that would normally be interpreted as wildcards? If we used backslashes to escape them, we'd

have to mark every single character. A short string would end up turning into:
*\?****\[a-b\]. Instead of doubling our amount of typing, we can use a pair of single quotes.

```
$ ls '*?****[a-b]'
*?****[a-b]
```

Any string encased in single quotes will not be modified by the shell, even when it's filled with wildcards.

INVERTING A WILDCARD

Sometimes you want every file in this directory *except* the ones that match a pattern. For example, you might have a directory with a few hundred files and about fifty of them follow no pattern in naming, but the other hundred and fifty do. If you could just invert what a wildcard looks for, you would have just what you need. That's where the "^", or caret modifier, and a set of square brackets comes in.

```
$ rm [^file_]*
```

The caret modifier turns the pattern over. It tells the shell to match all the filenames that *don't* match the pattern. There is one drawback to this trick, however, because only the asterisk wildcard can be specified outside the square brackets.

```
$ ls -1
file_1
file_2
...
file_100
random_file
more_random_file
file_xyz
$ rm [^file_]*
$ ls -1
file_1
file_2
...
file_100
file_xyz
```

In this case, since *file_xyz* matches the "file_" glob, it doesn't get expanded, so rm doesn't affect it.

12. SEARCHING FOR FILES

When you first get a computer, you tend to place files in just a couple folders or directories. But as your list of files grows, you have to create some subdirectories and spread the files around in order to keep your sanity. Eventually, you forget where files are. "Where did I store those photos I took in Normandy?"

You could run `ls -R`, as in the following section, and start running your finger down the screen, but why? Computers are supposed to be about automation. Let the computer figure out where the file is.

If you know your file is named "somefile", telling the computer what to do is pretty easy.

```
$ find . -name somefile -print
./files/somefile
```

The `find` command takes more arguments that the other commands we've seen so far, but if you use it for a while you'll find it becomes natural. Its first argument (the '.') tells find where to start looking: the directory at the top of everything you're searching through. In this case, we're telling `find` to start looking in whatever directory we're in right now.

The `-name` argument tells it to look for a file named *somefile*. Finally, the `-print` option tells the command to print out on our screen the location of any file that matches the name it was given.

WILDCARDS WITH FIND

What if you don't remember the name of the file you're looking for? You might only remember that it starts with "some". Luckily, `find` can handle that too.

```
$ find . -name 'some*' -print
./dir1/subdir2/files/somefile_other
./some_other_file
./files/somefile
```

This time it found a few more files than you were after but it still found the one you wanted. As you can see, the find command can process wildcards in much the same way the shell can. Here you asked it to look for anything that starts with the letters "some".

The "*", "?", and "[ ]" wildcards can all be used just as they would be in the shell. However, since find is using the wildcards you have to make sure they remain unaltered by the shell. To do this you can surround the name you're searching for, and the wildcards it contains, in single quotes.

TRIMMING THE SEARCH PATH

With just a name and a location, find will begin searching through every directory below its starting point, looking for matches. Depending on how many subdirectories you have where you're searching, find can take a lot of time to look in places you know don't contain the file.

It is possible, however, to control how far find sinks in the directory tree.

```
$ find . -maxdepth 1 -name 'some*' -print
./some_other_file
```

By using the -maxdepth argument we can tell find to go no lower than the number of directories we specify. A maxdepth of 1 says: don't leave the starting directory. A maxdepth of 3 would allow find to descend 3 directories from where it started, and so on. It's important to note that -maxdepth should immediately follow the start location, or find will complain.

USING CRITERIA

The find command can search for files based on any criteria the filesystem know about files. For instance, you can search for files based on:

- When they were last modified or accessed (somebody read them)
- How big they are
- Who owns them, or what group they are in
- What permissions (read, write, execute) they have
- What type of file (directory, regular file) they are

and other criteria described in the manual page. Here we'll just show a couple popular options.

The -mtime option shows the latest modification time. Suppose you just can't remember anything about a file's name, but know that you created or modified it within the past three days.

You can find all the files in your home directory that were created or modified within the past three days through:

```
$ find ~ -mtime -3 -print
```

Notice the minus sign before the 3, for "less than." If you know you created the file yesterday (between 24 and 48 hours ago), you can search for an exact day:

```
$ find ~ -mtime 1 -print
```

To find files that are more than 30 days old (caution: there will be a lot of these), use a plus sign:

```
$ find ~ -mtime +30 -print
```

Perhaps you want to remove old files that are large, before backing up a directory. Combine -mtime with -size to find these files. The file has to match all the criteria you specify in order to be printed.

```
$ find directory_to_backup  -mtime +30  -size +500k  -print
```

We've specified +500k as our -size option. The plus sign means "greater than" and "500k" means "500 kilobytes in size".

USING FIND TO RUN A COMMAND ON MULTIPLE FILES

The find command can do much more powerful things than print filenames. You can combine it with any other command you want, so that you can remove files, move them around, look for text in them, and so on. On those occasions, the find command with its -exec option is just what you'll need.

Because the next example is long, it is divided onto two lines, with a backslash at the end of the first so the shell keeps reading and keeps the two lines as one command. The first line is the same as the command to find old, large files in the previous section.

```
$ find directory_to_backup  -mtime +30  -size +500k -print \
        -exec rm {} \;
```

The -exec option is followed by an rm command, but there are two odd items after it:

- {} is a special convention in the -exec option that means "the current file that was found"
- \; is necessary to tell find what the end of the command is. A command can have any number of arguments. Think of -exec and \; as surrounding the command you want to execute.

So we find each file, print the name through -print (which we don't have to do, but we're curious to see what's being removed), and then remove it in the -exec option.

Clearly, a tiny mistake in a find command could lead to major losses of data when used with -exec. Test your commands on throw-away files first!

Using `cp` you can see how the bracket pairs can be specified multiple times, allowing the file's name to be easily duplicated.

```
$ find . -name 'file*' -exec cp {} {}.backup \;
```

Experiment and practice!

13. PIPING HOT COMMANDS

Pipes let programs work together by connecting the output from one to be the input for another. Pipes are built using a vertical bar ("|") as the pipe symbol.

Say you help your eccentric Aunt Hortense manage her private book collection. You have a file named *books* containing a list of her holdings, one per line, in the format "author:title", something like this:

```
$ cat books
Carroll, Lewis:Through the Looking-Glass
Shakespeare, William:Hamlet
Bartlett, John:Familiar Quotations
Mill, John Stuart:On Nature
London, Jack:John Barleycorn
Bunyan, John:Pilgrim's Progress, The
Defoe, Daniel:Robinson Crusoe
Mill, John Stuart:System of Logic, A
Milton, John:Paradise Lost
Johnson, Samuel:Lives of the Poets
Shakespeare, William:Julius Caesar
Mill, John Stuart:On Liberty
Bunyan, John:Saved by Grace
```

This is somewhat untidy, as they are in no particular order. But we can use the sort command to straighten that out:

```
$ sort books
Bartlett, John:Familiar Quotations
Bunyan, John:Pilgrim's Progress, The
Bunyan, John:Saved by Grace
Carroll, Lewis:Through the Looking-Glass
Defoe, Daniel:Robinson Crusoe
Johnson, Samuel:Lives of the Poets
London, Jack:John Barleycorn
Mill, John Stuart:On Liberty
Mill, John Stuart:On Nature
Mill, John Stuart:System of Logic, A
Milton, John:Paradise Lost
Shakespeare, William:Hamlet
Shakespeare, William:Julius Caesar
```

Ah, now you have a list nicely sorted by author. How about getting a list just of authors, without titles? You can do that with the cut command:

```
$ cut -d: -f1 books
Carroll, Lewis
Shakespeare, William
Bartlett, John
Mill, John Stuart
London, Jack
Bunyan, John
Defoe, Daniel
Mill, John Stuart
Milton, John
Johnson, Samuel
Shakespeare, William
Mill, John Stuart
Bunyan, John
```

A little explanation here. The −d option chose a colon as the delimiter (separator). This tells cut to break up each line wherever a delimiter appears, and each separate part of the line is called a field. In our format, the author's name appears as the first field, so we have put a 1 with the −f option to tell cut that we want to see just that field.

But you'll notice the list is unsorted again. Pipelines to the rescue!

```
$ sort books | cut -d: -f1
Bartlett, John
Bunyan, John
Bunyan, John
Carroll, Lewis
Defoe, Daniel
Johnson, Samuel
London, Jack
Mill, John Stuart
Mill, John Stuart
Mill, John Stuart
Milton, John
Shakespeare, William
Shakespeare, William
```

Voila! You've taken the alphabetized list, which is the output of the `sort` command, and fed it as input to the `cut` command. Don't give the `cut` command a filename to use, because you want it to operate on the text that's piped out of the `sort` command.

Pipes are just that simple--text flows down the pipe from one command to the next.

How about if you wanted a sorted list of titles instead? Since the title is the second field, let's try using −f2 with the `cut` command instead of −f1:

```
$ sort books | cut -d: -f2
Familiar Quotations
Pilgrim's Progress, The
Saved by Grace
Through the Looking-Glass
Robinson Crusoe
Lives of the Poets
John Barleycorn
On Liberty
On Nature
System of Logic, A
Paradise Lost
Hamlet
Julius Caesar
```

Oops. What happened? When looking at a pipeline, you need to go left-to-right. In this case, we sorted the file first before extracting the titles. So it dutifully sorted the lines starting with the author at the beginning of each line. To get the *titles* in the proper order, you need to do the sort *after* extracting them:

```
$ cut -d: -f2 books | sort
Familiar Quotations
Hamlet
John Barleycorn
Julius Caesar
Lives of the Poets
On Liberty
On Nature
Paradise Lost
Pilgrim's Progress, The
Robinson Crusoe
Saved by Grace
System of Logic, A
Through the Looking-Glass
```

Much better. Now this is all very nice, but you may be thinking you could have done these things with a spreadsheet. For simpler tasks, this is probably true. But suppose that Aunt Hortense is in the habit of asking odd questions about her collection. For example, she wants to know how many books she has from each author named John. A spreadsheet or other graphical program may have difficulty handling a request that wasn't anticipated by the program's authors. But the shell offers us many small, simple commands that can be combined in unforeseen ways to accomplish a complex task.

To find a particular string in a line of text, use the grep command. Now remember that when you combine commands, they need to go in the proper order. You can't run grep against the file first, because it will match the title "John Barleycorn" in addition to authors named John. So add it to the end of the pipeline:

```
$ cut -d: -f1 books | sort | grep "John"
Bartlett, John
Bunyan, John
Bunyan, John
Johnson, Samuel
Mill, John Stuart
Mill, John Stuart
Mill, John Stuart
Milton, John
```

This gets us close, but you don't want to get "Samuel Johnson" on the list and make Aunt Hortense angry. Often when working with grep you will need to refine the matching text to get exactly what you need. grep happens to offer a -w option that will let it match "John" only when "John" is a complete word, not when it's part of "Johnson". But we'll solve this particular dilemma by adding a comma and space on the front of the string to match, so it will match only when John is a first name:

```
$ cut -d: -f1 books | sort | grep ", John"
Bartlett, John
Bunyan, John
Bunyan, John
Mill, John Stuart
Mill, John Stuart
Mill, John Stuart
Milton, John
```

Ah, that's better. Now you just need to total up the number of books for each author. A little command called `uniq` will work nicely. It removes duplicate lines (duplicates must be on consecutive lines, so be sure your text is sorted first), and when used with the `-c` option also provides a count:

```
$ cut -d: -f1 books | sort | grep ", John" | uniq -c
      1 Bartlett, John
      2 Bunyan, John
      3 Mill, John Stuart
      1 Milton, John
```

And there you are! A nicely sorted list of Johns and the number of books from each. For our example set this is a simple job, one you could even do with pencil and paper. But this very same pipeline can be used to process far more data--it won't blink even if Aunt Hortense has hundreds of thousands of books stored in the barn.

System administrators often use pipelines like these to deal with log files generated by web and mail servers. Such files can grow to tens or hundreds of megabytes in size, and a command pipeline can be a quick way to generate summary statistics without trying to read through the entire log.

A nice thing about building pipelines is that you can do it one command at a time, seeing exactly what effect each one has on the output. This can help you discover when you might need to tweak options or rearrange the order of commands. For instance, to put the authors in ranking order, you can just add a `sort -nr` to the previous pipeline:

```
$ cut -d: -f1 books | sort | grep ", John" | uniq -c | sort -nr
      3 Mill, John Stuart
      2 Bunyan, John
      1 Milton, John
      1 Bartlett, John
```

Experiment!

14. PROCESSES

Processes are programs in action. Programs in binary/executable form reside on your disk; when they are executed (run), they are moved into memory and become a process. Each and every program we run is a process.

INTERRUPTING (CTRL-C)

Any process you are running in your shell can be stopped at any point while it is still running by pressing the **Ctrl** and **C** keys together. This shuts the process off almost immediately and you may lose data in any file it is writing (but it won't leave very important stuff half finished, like closing files).

PS AND KILL

We can use the ps and top commands to view processes running on our machine.

The ps command, when you run it without any arguments, displays processes run by the current user.

```
$ ps
  PID TTY          TIME CMD
 3922 tty2     00:00:00 su
 3923 tty2     00:00:00 sh
 3941 pts/0    00:00:00 cat
 3942 pts/0    00:00:00 ps
```

Here we find there are 4 processes that we are running from our terminal. The 4 columns have the following interpretation:

Process ID   Terminal   CPU Time   Program/Command

Each process has an identifier by which the operating system tracks it. This is an integer number that is given to each new process, and is called the PID (for "process ID"). The gap between the PID 3923 for sh and the PID 3941 for cat merely shows that somebody started processes on the machine in between the times these two processes started.

The second column in the output of `ps` specifies the terminal to which the process is attached or the terminal that controls the process. You can use the `tty` command to find out which terminal you are presently in.

```
$ tty
/dev/tty2
```

Now, you may well expect that your machine has a lot more processes than the ones you see by running a simple `ps` without arguments. In fact, it shows only the processes you started from the terminal in which you issue the command. On a graphical desktop, that command doesn't show the programs you start from menus or by clicking on icons. The system also runs a lot of its own processes in the background. To see everything, add the `-e` option:

```
$ ps -e
  PID TTY          TIME CMD
    1 ?        00:00:01 init
    2 ?        00:00:00 kthreadd
    3 ?        00:00:00 migration/0
    4 ?        00:00:00 ksoftirqd/0
    5 ?        00:00:00 watchdog/0
    6 ?        00:00:00 migration/1
    7 ?        00:00:00 ksoftirqd/1
    8 ?        00:00:00 watchdog/1
    9 ?        00:00:00 events/0
   10 ?        00:00:00 events/1
   11 ?        00:00:00 khelper
   44 ?        00:00:00 kblockd/0
   45 ?        00:00:00 kblockd/1
...........................................
...........................................
 3534 tty1     00:00:00 getty
 3535 tty2     00:00:00 login
 3536 tty3     00:00:00 getty
 3537 tty4     00:00:00 getty
 3538 tty5     00:00:00 getty
 3539 tty6     00:00:00 getty
```

In case you want to terminate a process that you started, you can do so from a terminal using the `kill` command.

```
$ kill 3941
```

Here we provide the PID as the argument. Remember that the kill argument is non-interactive (it doesn't ask for confirmation before starting) and non-verbose (it doesn't tell you what it is doing) by default and hence must be used carefully. You can kill only your own processes. Also if the program has truly crashed it may not respond to the instruction so use the -9 option in that case.

PROCESSES AND JOBS (BACKGROUND)

If you want to run something in the background and return control to your terminal, just put an ampersand ("&") after the command name.

```
$ firefox &
[1] 3694
$
```

The shell prints a brief message and gives you another dollar sign prompt. Firefox is now running (and should pop up a window of its own, because it's a graphical program). You can continue to execute other commands in your terminal.

What are the two numbers printed after you put the program in the background? The number in square brackets is a special number assigned to each program you run in the background; it's called a *job number*. In this case, the job number is 1 because we don't have any other programs currently running in the background in this shell.

The second number, which is 3694 in this case, is the process number we saw in an earlier section.

To bring your job back in the foreground just type fg. The job takes over your terminal as commands usually do, until it finishes.

If you have multiple jobs in the background, you can pass the job to the fg command either as a process number:

```
$ fg 3694
```

or as a job number:

```
$ fg %1
```

To distinguish the job number from a process number, you must put a percent sign ("%") before the job number.

If you want to run a process in the background that's now running in the foreground, type **Ctrl + Z**, which suspends the job, then issue the command bg.

To find out what jobs you've put in the background (and their status), enter jobs:

```
$ jobs
[1]-  Running                    firefox &
[2]+  Exit 2                     sort > big_file_sorted 2> big_file_err
```

Firefox is still running, but the second job exited with an error status of 2.

15. MORE ABOUT REDIRECTION

How do pipes work? They use three communication channels provided to every executing command.

stdin (standard input) is often what we type on the keyboard. We can use "<" with a filename to make a program take input from a file.

stdout (standard output) is often the text you see on your computer screen. We can use ">" to send that to a file, overwriting whatever is there, or we can use ">>" to append standard output to the end of the file.

stderr (standard error) is an alternative kind of output. Programs use it to send error messages. This can be useful because you might want to see error messages on the terminal even if you redirect output to a file. Here's an example:

```
$ ls *.bak > listfile
ls: *.bak: No such file or directory
```

Here, we wanted a list of all files ending in *.bak*. But no such files exist in this directory. If `ls` sent its error message to standard output (which in this case has been directed to a file), we wouldn't know what the problem is before looking at the content of *listfile*. But because `ls` sent its message to standard error, we see it. The error message starts with the name of the program (`ls`) followed by a colon and the actual message.

A pipe simply redirects the standard output of the first program to the standard input of the second:

```
$ ls *.bak | more
```

Sometimes, we want to direct the output of a command to a file, but we also want to see the output as the program runs. The `tee` command does just that:

```
$ ls -lR / | tee allMyFiles
```

provides a complete, detailed list of your file system, saved to *allMyFiles*. This takes some time to run; `tee` saves you from staring at a lifeless screen, wondering whether any thing's happening.

Each program can open a lot of files, and each has a number called a *file descriptor* that is meaningful only within that program. The first three numbers are always reserved for the file descriptors we just described.

stdin	0
stdout	I
stderr	2

REDIRECTING STDERR

Without using file numbers, error messages always go to your screen. For example

```
$ ls /nosuchplace > /dev/null
ls: /nosuchplace: No such file or directory
$
```

To change that you have to use the more general form of redirection, which uses the file numbers mentioned in the previous section, and looks like this.

```
$ ls /nosuchplace 2>/tmp/errors
$
```

This sends the error message sent to file number 2 (*stderr*) into the file */tmp/errors*.

Now we can introduce a more complex redirection, which redirects standard output and standard error to the same file:

```
$ ls *.bak > listfile 2>&1
```

The & in that command has nothing to do with putting a command in the background. The & here must directly follow the > character, and it sends file number 2 onto file number 1.

Or in the case of a pipe, put this before the pipe:

```
$ ls *.bak 2>&1 | more
```

ADDING MORE DESCRIPTORS

Sometimes it is convenient to keep other files open and add to them in dribs and drabs. You can do this with redirection and exec.

```
$ exec 3>/tmp/thirdfile
$ exec 4>/tmp/fourthfile
$ echo drib >&3
$ echo drab >&4
$ echo another drib >&3
$ echo another drab >&4
$ exec 3>&-
$ exec 4>&-
```

The first two lines open connections to two more file descriptors, 3 and 4. We can then echo text onto them, redirect programs into them, etc. using $>\&3$ or $>\&4$. Finally, we close them with the $3>\&-$ and $4>\&-$ syntax.

16. COMMAND HISTORY SHORTCUTS

The shell lets you bring back old commands and re-enter them, making changes if you want. This is one of the easiest and most efficient ways to cut down on typing, because repeated sequences of commands are very common. For instance, in the following sequence we're going through various directories, listing what's there, deleting files we don't want, and saving certain files under different names:

```
cd Pictures/
ls -l status.log.*
rm status.log.[3-5]
mv status.log.1 status.log.bak

cd ../Documents/
ls -l status.log*
rm status.log.[2-4]
mv status.log.1 status.log.bak

cd ../Videos/
ls -l status.log*
rm status.log.[2-5]
mv status.log.1 status.log.bak
```

Eventually, if you had to do this kind of clean-up regularly, you would write a script to automate it and perhaps use a cron job to run it at regular intervals. But for now, we'll just see how to drastically reduce the amount of typing you need while entering the commands manually.

An earlier chapter showed you how to use arrow keys to move around in your command history as if you were editing a file. This chapter shows a more complicated and older method of manipulating the command history. Sometimes you'll find the methods in this chapter easier, so it's worth practicing them. For instance, suppose you know you entered the mv command you want (or another one very similar to what you want) an hour ago. Pressing the back arrow repeatedly is a lot more trouble than recalling the command using the technique in this section.

RECALLING A COMMAND BY A STRING

The *bang operator*, named after the ! character (an exclamation point, or more colloquially "bang"), allows you to repeat recent commands in your history.

!string executes the most recent command that starts with *string*. Thus, to execute the exact same mv command you did before, enter:

```
!mv
```

What if you don't want the exact same command? What if you want to edit it slightly before executing it? Or just want to look at what the bang operator retrieves to make sure that's the command you want? You can retrieve it without executing it by adding `:p` (for "print"):

```
!mv:p
```

We'll show you how to edit commands soon.

Perhaps you issued a lot of mv commands, but you know there's a unique string in the middle of the command you want. Surround the string with ? characters, as follows:

```
!?log?
```

Entering two bangs in a row repeats the last run command. A very useful command history idiom is re-running the last command with superuser privilege:

```
sudo !!
```

as we all happen to type commands without the right permissions from time to time.

While running your last command may seem to have limited use, this method can be modified to select only portions of your last command, as we will see later.

RECALLING A COMMAND BY NUMBER

The shell numbers each command as it is executed, in order. If you like recalling commands by number, you should alter your prompt to include the number (a later chapter shows you how). You can also look at a list of commands with their numbers by executing the history command:

```
$ history
...
  502   cd Pictures/
  503   ls -l status.log*
  504   rm status.log.[3-5]
  505   mv status.log.1 status.log.bak
  506   cd ../Documents/
  507   history
$
```

Here we've shown only the last few lines of output. If you want to re-execute the most recent rm command (command number 504), you can do so by entering:

```
!504
```

But the numbers are probably more useful when you think backwards. For instance, if you remember that you entered the rm command followed by three more commands, you can re-execute the rm command through:

```
!-4
```

That tells the shell, "start where I am now, count back four commands, and execute the command at that point".

Repeating arguments

You'll often find yourself reusing portions of a previous command, either because you made a typo, or because you are running a sequence of commands for a certain task. We accomplish this using the bang operator with modifiers.

The three most useful modifiers are: *, !^, and !$, which are shortcuts for all, first, and last arguments respectively. Let's look at these in order.

"commandName *" executes the commandName with any arguments you used on your last command. This maybe useful if you make a spelling mistake. For example, if you typed emasc instead of emacs:

```
emasc /home/fred/mywork.java /tmp/testme.java
```

That obviously fails. What you can do now is type:

```
emacs !*
```

This executes emacs with the arguments that you last typed on the command-line. It is equivalent to typing:

```
emacs /home/fred/mywork.java /tmp/testme.java
```

"commandName !^" repeats the first argument.

```
emacs /home/fred/mywork.java /tmp/testme.java
svn commit !^    # equivalent to: svn commit /home/fred/mywork.java
```

"commandName !$" repeats the last argument.

```
mv /home/fred/downloads/sample_screen_config /home/fred/.screenrc
emacs !$    # equivalent to: emacs /home/fred/.screenrc
```

You can use these in conjunction as well. Say you typed:

```
mv mywork.java mywork.java.backup
```

when you really meant to make a copy. You can rectify that by running:

```
cp mywork.java.backup mywork.java
```

But since you are reusing the arguments in reverse, a useful shortcut would be:

```
cp !$ !^
```

For finer-grained control over arguments, you can use the double bang with the :N modifier to select the Nth argument. This is most useful when you are running a command with sudo, since your original command becomes the first argument. The example below demonstrates how to do it.

```
sudo cp /etc/apache2/sites-available/siteconfig /home/fred/siteconfig.bak
echo !^ !!:2  # equivalent to echo cp /etc/apache2/sites-available/siteconfig
```

A range is also possible with !!:M-N.

Editing arguments

Often you'll want to re-execute the previous command, but change one string within it. For instance, suppose you run a command on *file1*:

```
$ wc file1
    443    1578    9800 file1
```

Now you want to remove *file2*, which has a name very close to *file1*. You can use the last parameter of the previous command through "!$", but alter it as follows:

```
$ rm !$:s/1/2/
rm file2
```

That looks a little complicated, so let's take apart the argument:

```
!$    :   s/1/2/
```

The "!$" is followed by a colon and then a "s" command, standing for "substitute". Following that is the string you want to replace (1) and the string you want to put in its place (2) surrounded by slashes. The shell prints the command the way it interprets your input, then executes it.

Because this kind of substitution is so common, you'll be glad to hear there's a much simpler way to rerun a command with a minor change. You can change only one string in the command through this syntax:

```
$ wc file1
    443    1578    9800 file1
$ ^1^2
wc file2
```

We used a caret (^), the string we wanted to replace, another caret, and the string we want to put in its place.

SEARCHING THROUGH THE COMMAND HISTORY

Use the **Ctrl + R** key combination to perform a "reverse-i-search". For example, if you wanted to use the command you used the last time you used `snort`, start by typing **Ctrl + R**. In the terminal window you'll see:

```
(reverse-i-search)`':
```

As you type each letter (s, n, etc.) the shell displays the most recent command that has that string somewhere. When you finish typing "snort", you can use **Ctrl + R** repeatedly to search back through all commands containing "snort." When you find the command you're looking for, you can press the right or left arrow keys to place the command on an actual command line so you can edit it, or just press **Enter** to execute the command.

SHARING BASH HISTORY

The Bash shell saves your history so that you can recall commands from earlier sessions. But the history is saved only when you close the terminal. If you happen to be working in two terminals simultaneously, this means you can't share commands.

To fix this--if you want the terminal to save each command immediately after its execution--add the following lines to your ~/.bashrc file:

```
shopt -s histappend
PROMPT_COMMAND='history -a'
```

Learning these shortcuts can save you a tremendous amount of time so please experiment!

ADVANCED

17. PERMISSIONS
18. INTERACTIVE EDITING
19. CHECKING EXIT
20. SUB COMMANDS
21. MOVING AGAIN
22. CUSTOMISATION
23. PARAMETER SUBSTITUTION
24. GNUSCREEN
25. SSH
26. INSTALLING SOFTWARE

17. PERMISSIONS

Your computer system stores a lot of information about files that normally remains hidden as you create and play with the files. One set of file attributes you'll run into, though, is permissions. Who's able to edit your files? Hopefully not every person who logs in to the system (and many systems are still shared by multiple people nowadays). This section discussion ownership and permissions.

First, let's see what the system itself can tell us about its files. We'll execute the familiar `ls` command with an addition `-l` (that's the lower-case letter "L") option for a long listing:

```
$ ls -l
total 72
drwxr-xr-x   2 root root   4096 Oct  5 09:31 bin
drwxr-xr-x   3 root root   4096 Oct  9 21:47 boot
drwxr-xr-x   1 root root      0 Jan  1  1970 dev
...
```

The first line:

```
total 72
```

displays the total size of all the files together in *kilobytes* (kB). The rest provides information about the files and directories themselves. This information is grouped into seven columns that can be summarized as follows:

```
Permissions   Owner   Group   Links   Size   Date of modification   File Name
```

WHAT CAN I DO? WHAT CAN OTHERS DO?

Every file and directory in the system has an *owner*, belongs to a *group*, and has a set of *permissions* associated to it. At the simplest level, these permissions define three access levels, one for the owner of the file, one for the group that the file belongs to, and one for the rest of the world. (Actually, "world" just means anyone who has the privileges to log on to the system.)

Let's look back at the output shown previously. The third and fourth columns show the owner (root in this case) and group (root, too). The first column presents the permissions in a very compact fashion, like this:

```
drwxr-xr-x
```

The first character denotes the type of file, the next three characters show the owner permissions, the next three are the group permissions, and the last three are the permissions for the rest of the world.

The following table shows what the first character means. The previous example showed a "d" for directory. Some of the characters are quite rare. All you usually have to think about are the regular file and the directory.

Character	Description
-	regular file
d	directory
l	symbolic link
b	block special file
c	character special file
p	FIFO (named pipe)
s	socket
?	something else unknown to ls

Permissions are classified into 3 types:

- Read (r): permission to read a file
- Write (w): permission to write to a file
- Execute (x): permission to execute a file

If none of those permissions are set, a hyphen (-) appears in that position.

A simpler way to see how the permissions column is split up into their own columns is shown below:

```
:type : owner : group : restofworld:
:d    : rwx   : r-x   : r-x        :
```

If you wish to see the contents of a file, you need *read permission*. If you wish to modify its contents, you need *write permission*. If the file is a program and you wish to run it, you need *execute permission*.

In the case of directories, if you wish to see its contents, you need *both read and execute permissions*, just *read permissions* are not enough. If you wish to add or remove files from that directory, you need *write permissions*.

Going back to the example, let's consider the following line:

```
drwxr-xr-x   2 root root   4096 Oct   5 09:31 bin
```

As you now can see, it's a directory. How do you figure out what *you* can actually do with it? Here's where you need to look at the user and group assigned to the file. But first things first: who are you?

```
$ whoami
joe
```

That command will tell you just that: who you are, the name of your user account. As you can see, you are not *root*. The user *root* can see the contents of that directory and can also add files to it, but you are not him. What's your group then?

```
$ id -G -n
joe dialout cdrom floppy audio video plugdev
```

That's the list of groups you belong to. If any of those were *root* you'd be able to see the contents of the */bin* directory but not add files to it. But you are not part of the *root* group. The only option left is "the rest of the world" and you are included there, so what you can do is just see the contents of the directory.

Let's look at another file:

```
$ ls -l /etc/issue
-rw-r--r-- 1 root root 36 2009-02-26 15:06 /etc/issue
```

As you can see, it's a regular file that *root* can read and write and users in the *root* group, whoever they are, can only read. And you, *joe*, can only read it too.

What about your own stuff? Chances are you have a *Desktop* directory in your home directory. We'll check its permissions with ls -l, adding an extra -d option so we see just a line for *Desktop* and not the files or directories within it.

```
$ ls -l -d ~/Desktop
drwxr-xr-x 8 joe joe 4096 2009-03-12 09:27 /home/joe/Desktop
```

That directory belongs to you! And according to the permissions, you can read the contents and put files there. And other people can only look at its contents.

SETTING THROUGH CHMOD

If you wish to change permissions of a file, you need to own it--you can't just go around changing other people's stuff. If you own the file (or directory), you can change its permissions with the chmod command. There are two ways of specifying the new file's permissions and both have their advantages. Let's explore both.

Create a practice directory, and copy a couple of files there:

```
$ mkdir ~/practice
$ cd ~/practice
$ cp /etc/issue /etc/motd .
$ ls -l
 total 8
-rw-r--r-- 1 joe joe  36 2009-03-21 14:34 issue
-rw-r--r-- 1 joe joe 354 2009-03-21 14:34 motd
```

Let's say you wish to make *issue* readable and writable by you and your group only and *motd* readable and writeable by you only. That means the last output needs to look something like this:

```
$ ls -l
 total 8
-rw-rw---- 1 joe joe  36 2009-03-21 14:34 issue
-rw------- 1 joe joe 354 2009-03-21 14:34 motd
```

You take care of *issue* like this:

```
$ chmod u=rw,g=rw,o= issue
```

That means:

- u=rw: set the user's permissions to read/write
- g=rw: set the group's permission's to read/write
- o=: set the other's permissions to nothing

For *motd*, the command goes like this:

```
$ chmod u=rw,g=,o= motd
```

Pretty straightforward, isn't it? It's also a lot of typing. A shorter version would be:

```
$ chmod ug=rw,o= issue
$ chmod u=rw,go= motd
```

That's a little bit shorter, but there's an even shorter version:

```
$ chmod 0660 issue
```

That one needs a little bit of explaining. The numbers express the same permissions as before. If you want to understand how it works, consider the following diagram:

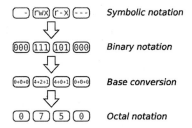

The top line shows us our goal: a file that its owner can read, write to, and execute, that its group can only read and execute, and that the rest of the world has no access to at all. Each letter in in the symbolic notation corresponds to a bit in the binary representation. If the letter is present, you have a 1 and if it's not you have a 0. The first 1 in 111 is 4, the second is 2 and the third is 1. You add all that up and you get 7. If you do the same for the other triplets, you get 0750.

Returning to our previous example, for the file *issue*, we wish to have the permissions be -rw-rw----, that gives us 0, 4+2, 4+2 and 0, that is 0660. Can you work out the *mode* (as this is called) for *motd*?

18. INTERACTIVE EDITING

Many people, especially beginners, use the arrow keys to move the cursor around the command line. However, this is painfully inefficient and should be avoided, since the bash shell offers much better ways to enter and edit commands. Most notably, the shell comes with two different sets of *key bindings* (keyboard shortcuts).

The two sets of bindings are inspired by two extremely powerful text editors, Emacs and vi (probably the two most powerful ones that exist). By exploiting the keyboard shortcuts that these bindings offer, command line wizards are able to enter and edit even long command lines in just a fraction of a second. If you take the time to practice with the key bindings that the shell offers, even if they may seem impractical at first, you will very soon be able to do so too.

Note: You will only be able to take full advantage of the Emacs and vi bindings if you know how to type properly (using 10 fingers). If you don't, you should learn it as soon as possible. (There are a lot of free sites on the web that can teach you.) It is definitely worth it.

By default, the bash shell uses the Emacs bindings. If you want to try out the vi bindings, enter the following command:

```
$ set -o vi
```

You can switch back to the Emacs bindings by entering:

```
$ set -o emacs
```

The Emacs and vi bindings are very different, and both take some time to get used to. You should try out both bindings to find the ones that suits you best. This chapter covers the default, Emacs bindings. If you learn vi, you can switch to those bindings and you will find them pretty intuitive.

Hint: Do not try to learn all shortcuts at once! The human brain isn't made for that kind of stuff, so you will forget almost all of them. Rather, we advise you to learn the 4-5 shortcuts that you find most useful and use them regularly -- learning by doing. Later, you can come back to this chapter to pick up more shortcuts. You will soon find yourself whirling across the command line.

THE EMACS BINDINGS

The Emacs bindings make heavy use of **Ctrl** and **Alt** as modifier keys. Experienced Emacs users usually remap their **CapsLock** key as **Ctrl** in order to enter Emacs commands more comfortably (and to avoid repetitive strain injury!). Once you start using the Emacs bindings on a regular basis, we advise you to do the same.

Moving around

The two most basic keystrokes for moving around on the command line in Emacs mode are **Ctrl + f** and **Ctrl + b**. They move the cursor one character to the right and to the left, respectively:

Ctrl + f	Move forward one character
Ctrl + b	Move backward one character

Of course, you can do the same cursor movements by using the arrow keys on your keyboard. But as was remarked above, using the Emacs bindings **Ctrl + f** and **Ctrl + b** is much more efficient, since your hands do not have to leave the letter block of your keyboard. At the moment, you may not notice the difference in speed (especially if you're not a fast typist yet), but once you get more experience in using the command line, you definitely won't want to touch the arrow keys again!

The following table lists some keystrokes which let you navigate the command line even faster:

Alt + f	Move forward one word
Alt + b	Move backward one word
Ctrl + a	Move to the beginning of the line
Ctrl + e	Move to the end of the line

Hint: The German word for "beginning" is Anfang. Would you ever forget such a strange word? Let's hope not, because it can help you remember that **Ctrl + a** takes you to the beginning of the command line.

By taking advantage of the keystrokes summarized in the table above, you can dramatically speed up your command line editing. If, for example, you have misspelled the first letter of a terribly long filename, the keystroke **Alt + b** brings the cursor back to the beginning of the word -- making cumbersome characterwise movement of the cursor unnecessary.

Editing text

Two of the most commonly used editing commands are the following:

Ctrl + t	Transpose the character before the cursor and the character under/following the cursor
Alt + t	Transpose the word before the cursor and the word under/following the cursor

The two commands take a while to get used to, but both are very useful. While the main use of **Ctrl + t** is to correct typos, **Alt + t** is often used to "drag" a word forward on the command line. Have a look at the following command line (the underline marks the position of the cursor):

```
$ echo one_two three four
```

If you press **Alt + t** in this situation, the word before the cursor ("one") is exchanged with the word after the cursor ("two"). Try it out! The result should look like this:

```
$ echo two one_three four
```

You will notice two things. First, the order of the words "one" and "two" has been reversed. Second, the cursor has moved forward along with the word "one". Now, the cool thing about the cursor's moving along is that you just need to press **Alt + t** once more in order to transpose "one" with the following word, "three":

```
$ echo two three one_four
```

So, by pressing **Alt + t** repeatedly, you can "drag" forward the word before the cursor until it has reached the end of the command line. (Of course, you can do the same with a single character by using **Ctrl + t**.)

At first, the elaborate functionality of the two transpose commands may seem a bit confusing. Just play around with them for a while, and you will soon get the hang of it.

Deleting/killing and reinserting text

Here are some handy commands for deleting/killing text:

Ctrl + d	Delete the character under the cursor
Alt + d	Kill all text from the cursor to the end of the current word
Alt + Backspace	Kill all text from the cursor to the beginning of the current word

Note that **Alt + d** and **Alt + Backspace** do not delete text, but kill it. Killing is different from deleting in that killed text may be reinserted (yanked) later on by using the following command:

Ctrl + y	Reinsert (yank) text that was previously killed

Let's see how this works by way of an example:

```
$ echo one two
```

Again, the cursor position is indicated by an underline. If you press **Alt + Backspace** in this
situation, the word "two" as well as the whitespace after it will be killed, leaving the command
line like this:

```
$ echo one
```

If you now press **Ctrl + y**, the killed text is "yanked" back into the command line. You can do this
several times. If you press **Ctrl + y** three times, for example, you end up with the following line:

```
$ echo one two two two
```

As you can see, killing text is much like the "cut" function of most modern text editors. Note
that text which is not killed, but deleted (by pressing **Ctrl + d**) cannot be reinserted into the
command line. The only way to get it back is to use the undo function, which will be introduced
below.

Probably the most useful commands for killing text are the following ones:

| Ctrl + k | Kill all text from the cursor to the end of the line |
| Ctrl + u | Kill all text from the cursor to the beginning of the line (unix-discard-line) |

As usual, the best way to learn these commands is to experiment with them. You will find that
killing and, where necessary, reinserting big stretches of text can save you a lot of time.

Undoing changes

You can undo the last change that you made by using the following command:

| Ctrl + _ | Undo last change |

An alternative way of doing the same thing is to press **Ctrl + xu**. (Press **x** and **u** in turn while
holding down **Ctrl**.)

Navigating the shell's history

The shell saves the last commands that you enter in its history. This allows you to get back to
previously entered commands, which can save you a lot of typing. Here are the most important
commands for navigating the shell's command history:

Ctrl + p	Go to the previous command in the history
Ctrl + n	Go to the next command in the history
Ctrl + >	Go to the end of the history

Ctrl + p	Go to the previous command in the history
Ctrl + r	Search the history for previously entered commands (reverse-search-history)
Ctrl + g	Cancel the current history search

Let's see how these commands work by way of a simple example. Open a shell and enter the following commands:

```
$ echo two
two
$ echo three
three
$ echo four
four
```

After you have entered these commands, you are left with an empty command line waiting for your input. Now, press **Ctrl + p**. You will notice that the previously entered command appears on your command line: echo four. If you press **Ctrl + p** once more, you move "up" in the history even further, so that echo three appears on the command line. Now, press **Ctrl + n**, and you will see that you have come back to echo four: **Ctrl + n** works exactly like **Ctrl + p**, but the other way round.

After having pressed **Ctrl + p** and maybe also **Ctrl + n** a few times, you may want to get back to the command line that you were entering before you started navigating the history. You can do this by pressing **Ctrl + >**.

As you can see, the shell's history is nothing else but a big list of all recently entered commands. You can move up and down the list by pressing **Ctrl + p** and **Ctrl + n**, respectively. And you can press the **Enter** key at any time in order to execute the currently selected command line.

Since the shell's command history is just a big list, it is also searchable. This is most commonly done by using the command **Ctrl + R**. Again, let's assume that you have entered the commands echo two, echo three and echo four. Try pressing **Ctrl + R** now. You will notice that a new prompt appears which says something like "reverse-i-search". If you now enter the letter "t", you immediately jump back in history to the last command line containing "t", which is of course **echo three**. From there, you can use **Ctrl + p** and **Ctrl + n** to navigate the history as explained above. Or you can modify the search by entering a second letter, let's say "w". You then jump to the command **echo two**, because it is the nearest command in history containing the letter sequence "tw". Or you can just cancel the search by pressing **Ctrl + g**.

If you feel a bit lost in using the shell's history functions, don't worry! If you keep on practicing, you will quickly get into the routine of flipping back and forth in the shell's history, avoiding the cumbersome retyping of long command lines.

Interactive editing: an example

The following example is intended to show you how the interactive editing capabilities of the shell can drastically speed up your work. Let's suppose you have entered the following command line:

```
$ echoo ne two three
bash: echoo: command not found
```

Bash has thrown an error, because the command *echoo* doesn't exist. What you really meant, of course, was *echo one two three*. You will perhaps be surprised to hear that it takes just five keystrokes to correct the mistake:

1. Press **Ctrl + p** to get the previous history item back on screen, namely the wrongly entered command line.
2. Press **Ctrl + a** to move the cursor to the beginning of the line.
3. Press **Alt + f** to move the cursor forward by one word. The cursor is now located between the wrongly entered words "echoo" and "ne".
4. Press **Ctrl + t**. You will see that the "o" preceding the cursor and the whitespace under the cursor have been transposed: "echoo ne" has become "echo one".
5. Finally, press **Enter** to execute the corrected command line.

19. EXIT STATUS

When you type commands, you can usually tell whether they worked or not. Commands that are unable to do what you asked usually print an error message. This is sufficient if you are typing in each command by hand and looking at the output, but sometimes (for example, if you are writing a script) you want to have your commands react differently when a command fails.

To facilitate this, when a command finishes it returns an *exit status*. The exit status is not normally displayed; instead it is placed in a variable (a named memory slot) named "**$?**". The exit status is a number between 0 and 255 (inclusive); zero means success, and any other value means a failure.

One way to see the exit status of a command is to use the `echo` command to display it:

```
$ echo "this works fine"
this works fine
$ echo $?
0
$ hhhhhh
bash: hhhhhh: command not found
$ echo $?
127
```

Now we'll look at various ways to handle errors.

IF/THEN

Handling an error is an example of something you do conditionally: *if* something happens, *then* you want to take action. The shell provides a compound command--a command that runs other commands--called `if`. The most basic form is:

```
if
  <command>
then
  <commands-if-successful>
fi
```

We will start with a basic example, then improve it to make it more useful. After we type `if` and press the **Enter** key, the shell knows we're in the middle of a compound command, so it displays a different prompt (**>**) to remind us of that.

```
$ if
> man ls
> then
> echo "You now know more about ls"
> fi
```
The manual page for ls scrolls by
```
You now know more about ls
```

Running this command brings up the manual page for `ls`. Upon quitting with the **q** key, the `man` command exits successfully and the `echo` command runs.

Handling command failure

Adding an `else` clause allows us to specify what to run on failure:

```
if
  <command>
then
  <commands-if-successful>
else
  <commands-if-failed>
fi
```

Let's run `apropos` if the `man` command fails.

```
$ if
> man draw
> then
> echo "You now know more about draw"
> else
> apropos draw
> fi
...
```

list of results for apropos draw

...

This time the man command failed because there is no draw command, activating the else clause.

&& AND ||

The if-then construct is very useful, but rather verbose for chaining together dependent commands. The "&&" *(and)* and "||" *(or)* operators provide a more compact format.

```
command1 && command2 [&& command3]...
```

The && operator links two commands together. The second command will run only if the first has an exit status of zero, that is, if the first command was successful. Multiple instances of the && operator can be used on the same line.

```
$ mkdir mylogs && cd mylogs && touch mail.log && chmod 0660 mail.log
```

Here is an example of multiple commands, each of which assume the prior one has run successfully. If we were to use the if-then construct to do this, we would have ended up with an unwieldy mass of ifs and thens.

Note that the && operator *short circuits*, that is, if one command fails, no subsequent command is run. We take advantage of this property to prevent unwanted effects (like creating *mail.log* in the wrong directory in the above example).

If && is the equivalent of then, the || *operator* is the equivalent of else. It provides us a mechanism to specify what command to run if the first fails.

```
command1 || command2 || command3 || ...
```

Each command in the chain will be run only if the previous command did not succeed (that is, had a nonzero exit status).

```
$ cd Desktop || mkdir Desktop || echo "Desktop directory not found and could not be c
```

In this example we try to enter the *Desktop* directory, failing which we create it, failing which we inform the user with an error message.

With this knowledge we can write an efficient and compact `helpme` function. Our previous examples have shown the two operators used in isolation, but they can be mixed as well.

```
$ function helpme() {
   man $1 && echo "you now know more about $1" || apropos $1
}
```

As you probably suspect, the "you now know..." echo is not exactly the most useful command. (It might not even be accurate, perhaps the `man` page introduced so many options and confused the poor user). We heartily confess we threw it in just to match the original if-then syntax. Now that we know about the || *operator*, we can simplify the function to:

```
$ function helpme() {
   man $1 || apropos $1
}
```

That covers the concept of exit status and using it to control the flow of your command and scripts. We hope you leave this chapter with an exit status of zero!

20. COMMAND SUBSTITUTION

In the shell, you can execute one command inside another. Here's a simple example:

```
grep `date +%b` apache_error_log
```

The **back-quote** key (also called the backtick) is usually located at the same place as the tilde, above the **Tab** key (dependent on your keyboard layout).

The command within the backticks `` is executed first. The output is then plugged into the larger command. So first the shell executes:

```
date +%b
```

This is the date command with an argument beginning with a + sign to indicate a format that you want for the output. The %b format is a rather odd convention asking the date command to print just a three-letter abbreviation of the current month. For instance, if we execute this command in March, it prints:

```
Mar
```

So the three-letter abbreviation of the current month is now inserted into the surrounding grep command. In the month of March, the command is equivalent to:

```
grep Mar apache_error_log
```

It just so happens that the *apache_error_log* file stores log messages with dates, and the date contains the three-letter abbreviation of the month:

```
[Mon Mar 09 14:44:23 2009] [notice] Apache/2.0.59 (Ubuntu) PHP/5.2.6 DAV/2 configured
```

So what is the effect of our command? It displays all the log messages from *apache_error_log* that were logged during the current month. (Of course, if there are multiple years in a single log file, you could get messages from March of previous years--but this example is meant to be simple.) By embedding the date command in the grep command, we have created a command we can store and execute any time without having to specify the right month. For instance, we could store this in the *.bashrc* start-up file:

```
alias monthlog="grep `date +%b` apache_error_log"
```

Now we have our very own command, `monthlog`, to display current Apache log messages.

In Bash, you can do the same thing with a syntax many people find simpler:

```
grep $(date +%b) apache_error_log
```

Instead of backticks, insert a dollar sign and put the command between parentheses.

Command substitution is like a pipe (the | character). But command substitution is more flexible than a pipe because you can put one command anywhere you want inside another. There is one other subtle difference: a pipe allows both commands to execute at the same time. If an embedded command takes a long time, the outer command doesn't execute at all until the embedded one is done.

If the embedded command could produce output that is more than one word (such as "Mar 09") you can pass it as a single argument by enclosing the command in double quotes. The `grep` command in this section, for instance, requires the string to be passed as a single argument.

21. MOVING AGAIN

So far you have probably already used the cd command to change your current working directory and the pwd command to find out what your current working directory is. After you work with the command line for a while, you'll find yourself changing directories constantly. In order to make this easier, Bash provides a "directory stack" that you can use to quickly move around directories where you are doing some work. (We'll show some examples in a moment that help explain the idea of a "stack.") You have the following commands at your disposal:

Command	Purpose
pushd dir	Push dir to the top of the stack and change the current working directory to it
pushd pushd +N	Switch the two top entries, changing back to the most recent directory (when entered without +N) Rotate N items on the stack, changing to the directory that comes out on top of the stack (when entered with +N)
popd	Remove the directory from the top of the stack and change the current working directory to the one at the top of the stack
dirs	Display the directory stack

If you need to have more of a visual aid to understanding a "stack", the simplest way is to imagine the "stack" as a pile of papers on your desk, you "push" new pieces of paper onto the top of the "stack" and you "pop" the top most piece of paper off the "stack". Both methods work on the principle of LIFO (last in first out).

You can play around with these commands to understand how they work. For example the following table provides a list of commands, their effect on the current working directory and their effect on the stack.

Command	Current working directory after command	Stack after command
cd	~	~

Command	Current working directory after command	Stack after command
pushd /	/	/ ~
pushd /usr/bin	/usr/bin	/usr/bin / ~
pushd +1	/	/ ~ /usr/bin
pushd +1	~	~ /usr/bin /
popd	/usr/bin	/usr/bin /
pushd +1	/	/ /usr/bin
popd	/usr/bin	/usr/bin

22. USEFUL CUSTOMIZATIONS

You can really make the shell your own, adapting every facet to the way your work (and even the different ways you work from week to week). In this section we'll look at quick changes you can make. Scripting, a way of really extending the functions offered by the shell, will be introduced later.

VARIABLES

Each command-line shell has the concept of a *variable*. Variables consist of two parts: the variable *name* and the variable *value*. If I were to say "x=6", "x" is the name of the variable, and "6" is the value. To see the value of a variable, one puts a dollar sign in front of the variable name. Here is a very simple example.

```
$ x=6
$ echo $x
6
$
```

Above, the first line *assigns* the value 6 to the variable x and the second line asks the shell to display the value of x. Note that we put the dollar sign in front of the variable name when we want to see its value, but we <u>never</u> use the dollar sign when assigning the value.

So anything starting with a dollar sign ($) is interpreted by the shell as a variable. One variable sneaked into an earlier section on exit status: you saw that **$?** contains the exit status of the previous command.

Now, what kind of useful things can we do with variables? A common use is to save typing. Say that the files for the project you're working on all week are located in a directory called */home/jsmith/projects/foo/confoobulator*. */home/jsmith/projects/foo/confoobulator* is a lot to type, but you can save typing by assigning the value to a variable.

```
$ p=/home/jsmith/projects/foo/confoobulator
```

Now you can change to my project directory by typing

```
$ cd $p
```

You can remove the value of a variable by setting it to an empty string:

```
$ VAR=""
```

or by issuing the unset builtin command:

```
$ unset VAR
```

ORDINARY VARIABLES AND ENVIRONMENT VARIABLES

Most shells (including the GNU bash shell) recognize two kinds of variables: *ordinary variables and environment variables*. An ordinary variable is available to your shell, but not to any programs that your shell runs. On the other hand, an environment variable is available to both your shell and all of the commands it runs. One can turn an ordinary variable into an environment variable by using the export command. If I were to type

```
$ export p
```

The (ordinary) variable **p** becomes an environment variable, and can be used by any command that my shell runs.

SHELL VARIABLES

The shell provides a lot of its own variables. For instance, the output of the whoami command (which was shown near the beginning of the book) is the same as $USER. Your home directory is stored in $HOME. You can see any variable's value by echoing it:

```
$ echo $HOME
```

The first dollar sign shown in that example is just a prompt; it has nothing to do with variables.

You can see the shell's built-in variables (actually a subset known as *environment* variables) through:

```
$ env
SHELL=/bin/bash
USER=jsmith
PATH=/usr/local/bin:/usr/bin:/bin:/usr/games
PWD=/home/jsmith
HOME=/home/smith
_=/usr/bin/env
...
```

Your output will look different, but many of the variable names will be the same. You will find some of these useful in later work.

- SHELL is the path to your login shell.
- USER is your username. When you logged into your GNU/Linux system, this is the username you typed in.
- PATH is a list of directories, separated by colons. When you run a command (like `cat` or `ls`), your shell looks in these directories to find the executable program. We'll talk more about PATH in just a moment.
- PWD is your current working directory (that is, the folder you are in).
- HOME is your home directory. You start out in this directory when you first log in.
- _ is the last executed command. In this case, /usr/bin/env.

CONTROLLING VARIABLE EXPANSION

If you jam a variable up against other characters, the shell won't recognize it. For instance, the following won't work:

```
$ curr=myfile
$ rm $curr1.jpeg
rm: .jpeg: No such file or directory
```

The error message could easily be perplexing. Here's what has happened: the shell saw a variable named **$curr1**. When it couldn't find any such variable, it substituted an empty string. So you ended up trying to execute:

```
$ rm .jpeg
```

If you want to remove *myfile1.jpeg*, use curly braces around the variable so the shell knows where the variable name ends:

```
$ rm ${curr}1.jpeg
```

THE SEARCH PATH

We've looked at several examples of running commands. If I type "ls -l" on the command line, then my shell runs the `ls` command, which list files. The `ls` command is actually a program sitting on your computer's hard drive. You can ask your shell where a command lives by using the `which` command. If I type

```
$ which ls
```

then my shell responds with "/bin/ls", which tells me the `ls` command is a program that lives in the /bin directory of my hard drive. We can even use the `ls` command to look at itself

```
$ ls -l /bin/ls
-rwxr-xr-x 1 root root 92672 2007-01-30 15:48 /bin/ls
```

My shell found the `ls` command by using the PATH environment variable.

```
PATH=/usr/local/bin:/usr/bin:/bin:/usr/games
```

The value of PATH is a list of directories, separated with colons. When I typed `ls`, my shell looked for the command in /usr/local/bin/ls, then /usr/bin/ls, and finally /bin/ls. /bin/ls is where the command lives, so my shell was able to run that. If there wasn't a /bin/ls, then my shell would have tried /usr/games/ls, and then given up.

CONFIGURATION FILES

You may have seen a lot of nice customizations in the book--or even better, thought up a few customizations of your own--and may be ready to save some of them so you can reuse them in every terminal session. Anything you define in the shell is lost when you close the terminal window. So this is a good time to look at configuration files, which save useful customizations between sessions.

Your home directory contains several hidden files that contain settings for the shell and other programs. In addition, there are entire hidden directories where programs store information, such as the colors you chose to put on your desktop.

How are these directories hidden? Through a simple convention: any file that begins with a dot (.) is considered hidden. Your file manager in your desktop won't show you the files unless you choose a special option to display hidden files. Similarly, the shell doesn't display them by default in an `ls` command. To display them in the shell, add the -a (for "all") option:

```
$ ls -a
.
..
.bash_history
.bash_logout
.bashrc
.irssi
.profile
foo
examplefile
```

In the previous listing (which will look different on your system) the *.bashrc* and *.profile* files are what we're particularly interested in. These are where you can put your customizations. It doesn't matter much which one you choose. The *.bashrc* file is particular to a type of shell (there are many types) called Bash, whereas *.profile* is read by other shells in case you decide to use something besides Bash.

Bash configuration works in a very simple manner: Bash just executes the commands when it starts up, exactly as if you typed them in before you did anything else. So anything you see in this section that you like--an alias, a function, a change to an environment variable, etc.--you can put in a configuration file. Entire scripts can be included.

Your startup files likely have commands in them already. Some are installed along with the operating system, while others are added by system administrators at workplaces. To change these customizations or add your own, check out the section on text editors in this book. Pick one editor and learn a dozen or so of its basic commands so you can do the minimal editing needed to put in your customizations.

FUNCTIONS

You can combine a number of commands and give it a name; then you can use this name like any other command. Consider writing a function whenever you find yourself executing the same commands repeatedly. You can also write flexible functions that change their behavior based on arguments, just as other commands do.

As a simple example, suppose you want to save information in a file each day:

```
echo ENTRY -------------- >>~/save/log
date >>~/save/log
du -c >>~/save/log
ls -R >>~/save/log
echo >>~/save/log
```

To save your commands as a function, issue a command named `function` followed by the name you want to assign it, and the commands in curly braces. Note that we've used hash marks (#) to add some comments so we will remember what the function is for later. The shell ignores the hash mark and any text that follows on that line.

```
function savelog {
# Add information about this directory a log file, ~/save/log
  echo ENTRY -------------- >>~/save/log
  date >>~/save/log
  du -c >>~/save/log  # Size of subdirectories
  ls -R >>~/save/log  # Complete file listing
  echo >>~/save/log
}
```

Now you can issue the command `savelog` and execute the embedded commands. You can put the function definition in a startup file so you never have to type the definition in again.

The previous example was quite contrived because you very rarely issue the exact same commands in sequence. However, you often have a complicated command that you run on different files, or other objects.

For instance, here is a command that shows you the differences between the current version of a file and the most recently edited version, if you edit with Emacs. Emacs saves an old version of your file by creating another file with the same name but an added tilde (~). In this example, we view the differences between *txtfile* and the back-up *txtfile~* version:

```
$ diff txtfile~ txtfile | less
```

This is just complicated enough (and common enough) to be worth saving as a function. But you want to pass the filename as an argument so you can use the function on any file you edit. So specify the argument as $1, a special variable that the function understands:

```
function d~ {
# Compare the Emacs back-up version with the current version.
  diff -u $1~ $1 | less
}
```

Now you can run your new d~ command on any file that has a backup:

```
$ d~ txtfile
```

As you might guess, a function can take up to nine arguments, which you can refer to as $1, $2, up to and including $9. If you want more than nine arguments, you can save an argument and remove it from the list:

```
function manyargs {
  $arg=$1
  shift
  . . .
}
```

The first thing this function does is save the first argument in its own **$arg** variable. The `shift` command removes the $1 argument and shifts all the other arguments over, so that the second argument is now $1. In the section on scripting, you'll see how to use loops to process arguments or other items one by one.

If you want to pass all the arguments to a command, use $*. For instance, the following `orth` function runs the spell utility on whatever string you pass:

```
function orth () {
  echo $* | spell
}
```

Functions can contains compound statements, such as if/then blocks. To show how flexible and powerful the combination of functions and compound statements can be, we'll include here an if/then statement that was shown earlier in the section "Handling command failure".

```
function helpme () {
  if man $1
    then echo "you now know more about $1"
    else apropos $1
  fi
}
```

So the following:

```
$ helpme draw
```

will now be equivalent to:

```
if man draw
   then echo "you now know more about draw"
   else apropos draw
fi .
```

As long as you can guess what errors or other conditions will occur, you can handle them automatically in a function.

SOURCING IN FILES

If this chapter has gotten you excited about the possibilities of writing up your customizations and saving them in files, good. But you will eventually have lots of different functions that fall into various categories, and you'll find it confusing to keep them all in one file. At this point, you can start storing commands, variable settings, and functions in various files that meet different needs, and read them into your *.bashrc* file or any other script. Just use a dot to read a file and have its contents executed by the shell:

```
.  scriptfile
```

It's important to put a space after the dot, before the filename.

SETTING PROMPTS

Whenever bash or any other shell is waiting for the user to type a command, it displays a prompt, which can be as simple or complex as you like. A minimal prompt would be

```
$
```

The default prompt looks something like

```
user@host:~$
```

where user is the login name, host is the name of the computer, ~ is the working directory, short for the user's home, typically in the form */home/user*, and $ means that the current user is not root.

To change the prompt, give a new value to the environment variable PS1. To make the change permanent, put the assignment in your *.profile* file, which bash reads whenever it starts up. The default value is \u@\h:\w\$, specifying username, host, working directory, and decorator characters. The following table describes the fields that can appear in a host, and various other useful characters. The prompt can ring the terminal "bell", now more usually a beep; it can contain multiple lines using \r for Carriage Return; and it can contain embedded terminal control sequences, typically starting with the Escape character. We will not attempt to explain all of these options here. See *Bash Reference Manual*, by Brian Fox and Chet Ramey, for full details. http://www.gnu.org/software/bash/manual/

\a	an ASCII bell character (07)	\d	the date in "Weekday Month Date" format (e.g., "Tue May 26")
\]	end a sequence of non-printing characters	\e	an ASCII escape character (033)
\h	the hostname up to the first '.'	\H	the hostname
\j	the number of jobs currently managed by the shell	\l	the basename of the shell's terminal device name
\n	newline	\r	carriage return
\s	the name of the shell, the basename of $0 (the portion following the final slash)	\t	the current time in 24-hour HH:MM:SS format
\T	the current time in 12-hour HH:MM:SS format	\@	the current time in 12-hour am/pm format
\A	the current time in 24-hour HH:MM format	\u	the username of the current user
\v	the version of bash (e.g., 2.00)	\V	the release of bash, version + patchelvel (e.g., 2.00.0)
\w	the current working directory	\W	the basename of the current working directory
\!	the history number of this command	\#	the command number of this command
\$	if the effective UID is 0 (root), a #, otherwise a $	\nnn	the character corresponding to the octal number nnn

\a	an ASCII bell character (07)	\d	the date in "Weekday Month Date" format (e.g., "Tue May 26")
\\	a backslash	\[	begin a sequence of non-printing characters, which could be used to embed a terminal control sequence into the prompt

Example:

```
$ PS1="\a\d, \t\r\n\u@\h:\w $"
```

would result in a sound from the computer, and the visible prompt

```
Mon Mar 23, 13:47:43
user@host:~ $
```

using \d for the date, \t for the time, \r\n for Carriage Return and New Line, and the rest as in the default.

To make things more interesting, you can run a program within the prompt by enclosing it in [\$( )]. This example counts the number of files in the current directory, by counting the lines (wc -l) piped in from a directory listing (ls).

```
$ PS1="\u@\h [\$(ls | wc -l)]:\$ "
user@host [3]:$
```

SUPERUSER PRIVILEGES

Besides the configuration files in each user's directory, the system has a lot of configuration files that control system-wide behavior. Sometimes you'll find it necessary to edit one by hand, using a text editor. In this section we'll show how to grant someone superuser privileges, a system-wide issue controlled by a file named /etc/sudoers.

It is best not to edit this file in an ordinary text editor. The sudoedit command provides a much safer way to edit configuration files.

```
$ sudoedit /etc/sudoers
```

This makes a temporary copy of the file and opens the copy in an editor. You can override the default editor by setting the VISUAL or EDITOR environment variable to "vi", "emacs", or whatever you like.

Permission lines in */etc/sudoers* identify the user, followed by the hosts the user can use `sudo` on, which groups the user can act as a member of, and which commands the user can execute using `sudo`.

An operator in a corporate or school system might have permissions that look like this.

```
operator      ALL = DUMPS, KILL, SHUTDOWN, HALT, REBOOT, PRINTING,\
                   sudoedit /etc/printcap, /usr/oper/bin/
```

(The '\' character continues the permissions on the next line.) This gives permission to run a specific set of commands, and to edit two specific configuration files, but no others. To give someone permission to run any superuser command using `sudo`, set the username's permission line to:

username `ALL = (ALL) ALL`

This also lets you edit any configuration file on your computer.

LOCALIZATION

Different countries use different conventions for all sorts of things: character sets, currencies, the formats of dates and times, and even paper size and shape. Computers can be instructed which language to use, and which version of the language to use for a particular country. This combination of customized information is called the *locale*.

All of the locale settings are reported by the `locale` command. For example,

```
$ locale
LANG=en_US.UTF-8
LC_CTYPE="en_US.UTF-8
LC_NUMERIC="en_US.UTF-8
LC_TIME="en_US.UTF-8"
LC_COLLATE="en_US.UTF-8"
LC_MONETARY="en_US.UTF-8"
LC_MESSAGES="en_US.UTF-8"
LC_PAPER="en_US.UTF-8"
LC_NAME="en_US.UTF-8"
LC_ADDRESS="en_US.UTF-8"
LC_TELEPHONE="en_US.UTF-8"
LC_MEASUREMENT="en_US.UTF-8"
LC_IDENTIFICATION="en_US.UTF-8"
LC_ALL=
```

The LANG setting **en_US.UTF-8** specifies English as the language, US as the country, and Unicode UTF-8 as the encoding. Money in the US is in dollars, $. Paper is letter, 8.5" × 11", as opposed to A4 for most of the rest of the world.

You usually specify a language and country when you install your operating system, and everything including the shell picks those values up. Originally, it was supposed that language, country, and character encoding would go together, but in our increasingly global society, it can happen that a Hungarian temporarily in the US on UN business would choose UTF-8, French language, metric (SI) measurements, Euros, Swiss address and telephone formats (for the home office in Geneva), and US letter paper.

You can change any of these settings in your shell by assigning an appropriate string to the relevant environment variable. The accepted values for locale settings are provided with options to the locale command.

```
$ locale -m # available charmaps: character set and encoding identifiers
ANSI_X3.110-1983
ANSI_X3.4-1968
ARMSCII-8
ASMO_449
BIG5
BIG5-HKSCS
...          # 226 choices in Ubuntu 8.10

$ locale -a # available locales for English and UTF-8 in various countries
C
en_AU.utf8
en_BW.utf8
en_CA.utf8
en_DK.utf8
en_GB.utf8
en_HK.utf8
en_IE.utf8
en_IN
en_NG
en_NZ.utf8
en_PH.utf8
en_SG.utf8
en_US.utf8
en_ZA.utf8
en_ZW.utf8
POSIX
```

You will get different locale specifications depending on the languages and encodings selected on your system at installation time or modified later.

To set your preferences, check for the correct format using these commands, and set the locale environment values in your *.profile* accordingly.

Another essential element of localization is your preferred keyboard layout, set with the loadkeys command for the command line, and setxkbmap for the X Window System (used on virtually all free desktops).

```
$ loadkeys de-latin1 # German
```

or

```
$ setxkbmap dvorak # Dvorak keyboard for English
```

The setfont command lets you change to a font for a specific writing system.

```
$ setfont iso01.f16
```

This sets a bitmap font covering ISO 8859-1, suitable for many Western European languages.

If you need to type documents in more than one writing system, you probably need to move to X. But there are extended versions of Emacs and vim that can create plain text files in multiple writing systems, either in their own format or in Unicode.

23. PARAMETER SUBSTITUTION

As we saw in the chapter on variables, you can put braces around a variable name to set it off from its surroundings:

```
$ curr=myfile
$ rm ${curr}.jpeg
```

There are also some nifty tricks you can perform inside the braces, such as changing parts of the string. Suppose you have a file named *mypicture.jpeg* instead of *myfile.jpeg*. You could alter the $curr variable when you insert it into a command:

```
$ rm ${curr/file/picture}.jpeg
```

PLAYING SAFE WITH VARIABLES THAT DON'T EXIST

Sometimes you might be using variables that have been removed (which you can do with the unset command) or were never initialized in the first place. Since by default the shell uses an empty string for a nonexistent or undefined variable, as in the case of the rm command we showed earlier, it's useful to be able to substitute a default value for a variable.

```
$ cat "${VARIABLE_FILE_NAME:-/home/user/file}"
```

The ':-' operator asks the shell to check whether the variable is set. to see if it exists and is set to some string. If it was never defined, or has no value, the shell substitutes the text after ':-'.

```
$ cat "${VARIABLE_FILE_NAME:=/home/user/file}"
```

The ':=' operator will do much the same, but instead of just substituting */home/user/file* in the current cat command, if VARIABLE_FILE_NAME doesn't exist, the shell will also set the variable to the alternative text.

CUTTING CORNERS WITH VARIABLE EXPANSION

Variable expansion is by no means limited to filenames. It is also a handy way to pass complex, frequently used options to commands.

```
$ export ALT_LS='--color=always -b -h --filetype'
$ ls $ALT_LS
```

Since the alternative options are stored and expanded in variable form, you can use whatever defaults you like for ninety-percent of your work but quickly use an alternative form in special cases.

Parameter expansion is an excellent way to abstractly deal with multiple files or tediously long series of options. Once you understand it, it's bound to expand your abilities on the command line.

24. GNU SCREEN

GNU Screen helps you get most out of your desktop's real estate, in cases where you need to work on more than one terminal simultaneously. Using GNU Screen, you can have as many processes as you need, such as editors, web browsers and shells, all within a single terminal window. Every desktop system allows you to open multiple terminals in different windows, and most terminal programs let you run multiple sessions at once using tabs, but GNU Screen is often easier to manage and less confusing when you have many sessions. Additionally, GNU Screen offers a copy-paste mechanism to transfer pieces of text easily within the multiplicity of sessions handled by it.

Start by typing `screen` in your command prompt.

```
$ screen
```

You get a welcoming message and some versioning information.

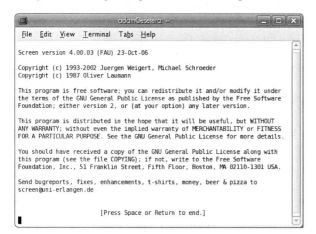

If you press **Enter** you get a shell prompt, just like before you invoked Screen. You are now running within a single session of Screen. In order to create a second session with its own shell, press **ctrl + a** followed by **c** (release the **ctrl** key before pressing the **c**). You now go to a new shell.

If you want to run just one command in a new screen and then close the screen, specify the command as an argument:

```
$ screen irssi
```

SWITCHING SESSIONS

To switch to the previous shell, enter **ctrl + a** followed by the **p** key. To go forward again, enter **ctrl + a** followed by the **n** key. You can see a list of all the sessions you have created using **ctrl + a** followed by the **"** key. This presents a scroll-down menu listing all open sessions (very helpful when you have created many sessions!). If you want to save even the half second it takes to scroll down the menu, while being able to see a list of available sessions and instantly jump to another session, enter **ctrl + a w**. This keeps you in your current window, but adds, at the bottom of the screen, a list of sessions with a different number for each. Then enter **ctrl + a** *session_number* to jump to the session of your choice.

Suppose you created a few sessions under GNU screen. In one session you have a Vim editor open, a couple more sessions you use for logging in to different remote servers, another session you use to run FTP, and so forth. By default, **ctrl + a "** shows the program you used to start each session. Normally you started it with the shell, so **ctrl + a "** shows "bash" for each session (or whatever your shell is). This isn't very helpful if you want to quickly find the session that's running Vim or FTP.

It turns out that customizing the display is easy. While you are in a session--say, editing in vim--press **ctrl + a** A and you get a line at the bottom of your window with the name of your session, which you can edit to your liking.

COPY & PASTE

Now say you are creating a shell script within Vim, and you want to test a single line from it containing a few shell commands to see how they would actually behave when run in a shell. That means you want to copy the text from the Vim screen and paste it in a Bash shell prompt. With GNU Screen, you can do this easily.

1. While in your vim session, press **ctrl + a [** to put you in *screen copying* mode.
2. Navigate through the text anywhere in your window using Vim positioning commands. After you get to the line of interest, press the **spacebar**.
3. Select specific lines to be copied by simply moving though the text using Vim's positioning commands until you reach the end of what you want to copy (text is highlighted as you proceed with your selection).
4. Once you finish selecting text, press the **spacebar** again to copy the text to the clipboard.
5. Using the session switching commands described earlier, navigate to a session containing a Bash shell and press **ctrl + a]**. This pastes the selected text, which in this example are some

shell commands, right into the Bash command line.

In this way you can very easily test your commands, then go back to the Vim session to edit and save your shell script.

SPLITTING THE SCREEN

Besides multiple full-screen windows, Screen can also allow two or more programs to share the screen at once.

Use **ctrl + a S** (capital S) to divide your screen into two parts. Your original session is at the top and a new blank session at the bottom. (Be careful you don't accidentally press **ctrl + s**. This can lock up your terminal. If you do accidentally hit **ctrl + s**, you can unlock the terminal with **ctrl + q**.) By default, there is no program running in this new region, but you can start one by using **ctrl + tab** to move to that region and then typing **ctrl + a c**.

Each region acts as an independent session, and you can switch between sessions just as in fullscreen mode.

You can remove the current region by using **ctrl + a X**. This won't destroy the session or what's running in it. It just turns the other session back into a full-sized window.

DETACHING A SESSION

One of Screen's most powerful features is the ability to halt and restore sessions. Say you're doing something really interesting on your computer, but you have to leave and go to work. Now say that while away you want to access what you were working on. If both machines are accessible through the Internet, you can do that with Screen.

Type **ctrl + a d** in your screen session. You return to your original terminal and the screen exits, printing **[detached]**. Now if you execute ps, you find that the screen is still running in the background. Get a list of all running sessions by passing screen the -list option.

```
$ screen -list
There is a screen on:
12056.pts-0.hostname
(Detached)
1 Socket in
/var/run/screen/S-user_name.
$
```

You can reconnect to this running session by entering:

```
$ screen -r 12056.pts-0.hostname
```

Or you can just use:

```
$ screen -R
```

This reconnects to the first session it finds.

Now all you have to do is log into your home machine from any remote machine and you are able to see whatever you were working on, exactly as you left it. Use the same procedure to put a download into the background with `wget`, or `ftp`. A detached session persists even if you log out from the machine.

QUITTING SCREEN

If you have only a few programs open, you can exit screen simply by quitting them all. However, if you have many different application and windows open, you can exit them all by typing **ctrl + a** \. You are prompted for confirmation, and if you select yes, Screen terminates all its programs and exits.

25. SSH

The command line is such a useful tool that it won't be long before you need to have access to the command line on a computer that is not sitting in front of you. In the old days, before security was a concern, people used `telnet` to get a command line on a remote computer. For most purposes, `telnet` is no longer a good idea, because data is transmitted in a raw, unencrypted format. The standard secure way to gain access to a command line on a remote computer is via `ssh` (secure shell). The simplest invocation of the command is

```
$ ssh othermachine.domain.org
```

This command assumes that your username on the remote machine is the same as your username on the local machine at which you type the command. The remote machine prompts you for your password. If your username on the remote machine is different than your username on the local machine, use the `-l` (lower-case "L") option to indicate your username on the remote machine.

```
$ ssh -l remoteusername othermachine.domain.org
```

Alternatively, you can use email-style notation to indicate a different username.

```
$ ssh remoteusername@othermachine.domain.org
```

So far, all these commands display a command line on the remote machine from which you can then execute whatever commands that machine provides to you. Sometimes you may want to execute a single command on a remote machine, returning afterward to the command line on your local machine. This can be achieved by placing the command to be executed by the remote machine in single quotes.

```
$ ssh remoteusername@othermachine.domain.org 'mkdir /home/myname/newdir'
```

`ssh` offers many other options, which are described on the manual page. You can also set up your favorite systems to allow you to log in or run commands without specifying your password each time. The setup is complicated but can save you a lot of typing; try doing some Web searches for "ssh-keygen", "ssh-add", and "authorized_keys".

SCP: FILE COPYING

The SSH protocol extends beyond the basic `ssh` command. A particularly useful command based on the SSH protocol is `scp`, the secure copy command. The following example copies a file from the current directory on your local machine to the directory */home/me/stuff* on a remote machine.

```
$ scp myprog.py me@othermachine.domain.org:/home/me/stuff
```

Be warned that the command will overwrite any file that's already present with the name */home/me/stuff/myprog.py*. (Or you'll get an error message if there's a file of that name and you don't have the privilege to overwrite it.) If */home/me* is your home directory, the target directory can be abbreviated.

```
$ scp myprog.py me@othermachine.domain.org:stuff
```

You can just as easily copy in the other direction: from the remote machine to your local one.

```
$ scp me@othermachine.domain.org:docs/interview.txt yesterday-interview.txt
```

The file on the remote machine is *interview.txt* in the *docs* subdirectory of your home directory. The file will be copied to *yesterday-interview.txt* in the home directory of your local system

`scp` can be used to copy a file from one remote machine to another.

```
$ scp user1@host1:file1 user2@host2:otherdir
```

To recursively copy all of the files and subdirectories in a directory, use the `-r` option.

```
$ scp -r user1@host1:dir1 user2@host2:dir2
```

See the `scp` man page for more options.

RSYNC: AUTOMATED BULK TRANSFERS AND BACKUPS

`rsync` is a very useful command that keeps a remote directory in sync with a local directory. We mention it here because it's a useful command-line way to do networking, like `ssh`, and because the SSH protocol is recommended as the underlying transmission for `rsync`.

The following is a simple and useful example. It copies files from your local */home/myname/docs* directory to a directory named *backup/* in your home directory on the system *quantum.example.edu*. `rsync` actually minimizes the amount of copying necessary through various sophisticated checks.

```
$ rsync -e ssh -a /home/myname/docs me@quantum.example.edu:backup/
```

The `-e` option to `ssh` uses the SSH protocol underneath for transmission, as recommended. The `-a` option (which stands for "archive") copies everything within the specified directory. If you want to delete the files on the local system as they're copied, include a `--delete` option. See the `rsync` manual page for more details about `rsync`.

MAKING LIFE EASIER WHEN YOU USE SSH OFTEN

If you use SSH to connect to a lot of different servers, you will often make mistakes by mistyping usernames or even host names (imagine trying to remember 20 different username/host combinations). Thankfully, SSH offers a simple method to manage session information through a configuration file.

The configuration file is hidden in your home directory under the directory *.ssh* (the full path would be something like */home/jsmith/.ssh/config* --if this file does not exist you can create it). Use your favorite editor to open this file and specify hosts like this:

```
Host dev
HostName example.com
User fc
```

You can set up multiple hosts like this in your configuration file, and after you have saved it, connect to the host you called "dev" by running the following command.

```
$ ssh dev
```

Remember, the more often you use these commands the more time you save.

26. INSTALLING SOFTWARE

Installing software on GNU/Linux is a broad subject because each version of GNU/Linux has its own way of doing things. Most are variations on apt-get (Advanced Packaging Tool), used by Debian, Ubuntu, gNewSense, and related distributions) or yum (Yellowdog Update Manager), used by Fedora, BLAG, and related distributions. The basic syntax is

```
$ sudo apt-get install packagename
$ sudo yum install packagename
```

Several apt-get and yum functions have the same name and act in the same way, but by no means all. When you want to go beyond the simple cases described here, be sure to check the documentation for whichever you are using.

These examples use sudo to remind you that installing software and editing configuration files require superuser privileges. You can either use sudo with each command, or switch to being superuser with the su command. (Remember to exit your superuser session before resuming normal user work.)

There are numerous options to each command. To uninstall a package, use this command.

```
$ sudo apt-get remove packagename
$ sudo yum remove packagename
```

To read repository index files, and update the local package database.

```
$ sudo apt-get update
$ sudo yum update
```

To install all available newer versions of packages.

```
$ sudo apt-get upgrade
```

To fix broken dependencies, if any.

```
$ sudo apt-get --fix-broken
```

The yum command does not have this option. There are other ways to deal with broken RPM package dependencies, but they require more help than we can give you here.

Users can configure multiple package repositories to download from by editing */etc/apt/sources.list* as superuser. Be careful. Back up the current file before making any changes.

All types of GNU/Linux allow the user to install software using the source code. For software in Debian-style packages, you can use

```
$ apt-get source packagename
```

The yum utility does not handle source installs.

Compiling from source is especially important for software that is not available in packages, typically because it is too new. You probably don't want to tackle this process unless you know a little bit about how to use GNU/Linux commands and a little about the GNU/Linux file system, but whenever you decide to try out something brand new and possibly unfinished, this is the most common method. If you don't know about commands and file systems, you can easily get lost doing a source code installation. It is better to read up on them first, get comfortable with them, and then return here.

Installing from source works on any GNU/Linux system, so it's a good process to know, and it more or less follows this route once you have a source package:

1. Unpack the archive and cd to its base directory.
2. Run the configure script **./configure**
3. Compile the software **make**
4. Install the software **make install**

To carry out the second and third steps, you must have compiler tools on your system. Some GNU/Linux systems come with these tools automatically, but others do not. Any system you are likely to use with this book, though, allows you to download the tools you need for free; search for the packages containing gcc and binutils.

DEPENDENCIES

Before we start, a word on dependencies. GNU/Linux developers often don't write an application from scratch; they rely heavily on work that has been done previously by other programmers. This is a smart practice, of course, because it saves time, and to aid this process many kind-hearted individuals have made libraries of code that other programmers can easily access and use within their own programs. These libraries are stored in fixed places in the GNU/Linux file system, usually in the directories whose names begin with */lib*, */usr/lib*, and */usr/share/lib*.

If you install an application that requires certain libraries, it's easy as long as you have those libraries already installed on your system. However, if you don't have the required libraries, you need to find them and install them. If the programmers are thoughtful, they will have included information about dependencies in either the *README* or *INSTALL* files that you will find in the source directory of the application. Some extremely nice programmers give you both the name and the URL where you can get the necessary bits.

However, if you are installing software on a distribution other than the one it was developed on, you are likely to find libraries packaged quite differently than on the developer's system. In this case you may have to use the trial and error method: try compiling the source, and when you get an error message telling you of a missing dependency, try to install it. If you can't install it using the name given, you may need to ask someone more experienced how to find the appropriate package, or go looking for documentation of your distribution's packaging policies.

Usually, lazy GNU/Linux users don't bother to read these files so they just go through the standard process and find that the configure stage will give an error telling them what libraries are missing. These lazy types (this author included) then find the required bits and pieces online and install them.

However, if you are new to GNU/Linux, I suggest that you read the *README* and *INSTALL* before starting any installation process. It will save you time and heartache.

Just remember that although a dependency list might be long, you simply get all the necessary packages and install them one by one, following the same process described in the previous section, until finally you have everything you need for the program of your dreams to install and run.

Next, let's look at the installation process a little more in depth.

UNPACK THE ARCHIVE

Most software sources come in the form of a compressed tar archive. You can recognize these archives by the suffix ".tar". They are also usually compressed as well. The GNU `tar` command can automatically uncompress files ending with a *.gz* or *.tgz* suffix (which means the distributor used GZIP compression) but if other forms of compression were used (such as BZIP2 or LZMA) you have to use the appropriate uncompression program to retrieve the *.tar* file (colloquially known as a *tar ball*). To unpack the archive, use the `tar` command:

```
$ tar zxvf packagename.tar.gz
```

Where "packagename" in the example above is the actual name of your package that you wish to install. The `tar` command followed by the parameters `zxvf` uncompresses a *tar.gz* file and creates a new directory with all the extracted sources. You can remove the *tar.gz* file after it successfully unpacks.

Now you must change your working directory to this new directory using the `cd` command. Usually the new directory name is the name of the compressed source package minus the *.tar.gz* suffix. For example, if my package really was called *newsoftpack-1.0-alpha.tar.gz*, then after running the `tar zxvf` command on it I would be left with a new directory called *newsoftpack-1.0-alpha* and would type `cd newsoftpack-1.0-alpha` to enter this new directory. If you are not sure of the name of the newly created directory, type `ls`.

RUN THE CONFIGURE SCRIPT

Once inside the new directory, we want to start the actual installation process. To do this, most of the time you will need to type the following:

```
$ ./configure
```

Properly packaged source distributions usually contain a script that prepares the source tree for building and installation. In this case, we will assume that it is `configure`, since it is a very popular choice for such a script. Sometimes, the command you need to use is different. In those cases, look for information in the *README* or *INSTALL* file.

In the command shown, by putting a dot and a slash before the name of the script (`./configure`) you are telling GNU/Linux to execute (run) a script called `configure` from the current directory (denoted by "`./`"). The script then does its stuff, checking what kind of a computer you have, what you already have installed, what kind of GNU/Linux you are running, and so on.

One option to `configure` is particularly common: the `--prefix` option, which tells `configure` you want the software installed in a non-default location. On most systems, the default is fine, and it may be where other software expects to find the software or library you're installing. But sometimes you can't install the software into a shared location or you want it somewhere under your own home directory because you know you're the only person using it. To change the directory where the software will ultimately be installed, specify it with `--prefix`:

```
$ ./configure --prefix ~/bin/myprogs
```

The most common problem that will occur at this stage is that the configure script will halt and tell you that some software library that the new software depends on is missing. If you do experience this error, check the *README* and *INSTALL* files in case they tell you how to repair the problem, then use a search engine if necessary to find out what software the error message is talking about and where to get it. Then start the installation process again with this new package. This means that an installation sometimes can take days while you search and download all the packages you need. This is one of the great advantages of package management systems such as yum and apt-get: when developers create packages for these systems, they automate the installation of dependencies.

In some cases, dependencies are optional. The `configure` script actually supports a lot of options. You can see what options your software package supports by running:

```
$ ./configure --help
```

COMPILE THE SOFTWARE

Assuming the `configure` process finished successfully, the next command to type in the installation process is:

```
$ make
```

If you have several processors or processor cores, you can use multiple jobs to speed up processing by adding a `-j` option:

```
$ make -j3
```

These commands actually make ("compile") the software for you. You will then end up with a whole lot of compiled files which in total makes up your software. The `make` process can take a while, depending on the speed of your machine and the size of the package sources you are installing. Running other processor-intensive applications will also slow down the process.

In the second command shown, `-j3` tells `make` to try to run 3 compilation processes simultaneously, which will allow you to utilize processor resources better if you have a dual-core or bigger machine. The number after `-j` is arbitrary, but a good rule of thumb is the number of processor cores plus one.

As with `configure`, you may encounter errors during compilation. In such a case, if you can't fix the problem yourself, contact the developer of the software and politely ask for help, explaining your problem very clearly. The Web page http://www.catb.org/~esr/faqs/smart-questions.html explains how to write polite and helpful problem reports.

INSTALL THE SOFTWARE

After `make` has stopped without errors, type the following:

```
$ sudo make install
```

This will install the newly created files from your software in the correct locations in your system. This is usually under /usr/local/, though this can be overridden with a `configure` option, as we have seen. Because software is usually installed in a shared directory that only the root user can write to, you need to start the command with `sudo` to have permission to add your software. You don't need the `sudo` if you told `configure` to install into a directory under your own home directory.

So now you just need to type the name of the application in your terminal window and it should run. If it fails to start, a common remedy is to type `ldconfig` and then try again. `ldconfig` updates the system so that your operating system knows that there are new library files present.

TEXT EDITORS

27. TEXT EDITORS

Besides running simple commands like `ls` and `grep`, you can use the command line to start large, complex programs. Before graphical interfaces were common, programs were designed to use plain text and take up the screen. Now these programs run within the same window that you use for the command line.

In this book we'll focus on text editors, because you need them to save your commands for later use and to write scripts. They're handy for lots of other things too; for instance, you may want to edit HTML files on a web server using a text editor.

WORD PROCESSING VS TEXT EDITING

Almost everybody who uses a computer is familiar with a word processor. The free software world provides several powerful ones, including OpenOffice.org and KWrite. The text editors we show in this book manipulate text, like word processors, but there's a fundamental difference.

- Word processors store a lot more than a stream of text characters you see on the screen. They want to provide "rich text," with italic and bold, numbering and bullets, colors--you name it. This is obviously valuable for many purposes. A plain text resume does not impress many employers.
- On the other hand, word processors are showing their limitations these days: some word processors have proprietary formats that make it hard to use documents in other programs. In fact, sometimes you cannot open a document with another version of the same word processor, or the document has display problems.
- Many people find online collaboration tools (such as the wiki software we used to write this manual) and content management systems (such as many weblog sites use) easier for modern document production than a word processor. But word processors are also evolving to do a better job supporting collaboration; probably all these tools will merge over time and evolve into something better than any of them offered before.

Word processors, wikis, content management systems, and text editors all have their place. The tasks in this book require a text editor. If you want to use a word processor to edit these files, you can do so, but make sure to choose a plain text form when you save the file.

WHY DO YOU NEED A TEXT EDITOR?

GNU/Linux is a very file-centric operating system: everything is (or looks like) a file. All basic configuration is done via carefully crafted text files, in the right place with the right contents. You can find many graphical tools to configure your GNU/Linux box, but most of them just tweak text files on your behalf.

Those text files have an exact syntax that you must follow. A simple misplaced character could jeopardize your system, so using a word processor for this matter is not only a bad idea but could corrupt your files with extra formatting information. Configuration files don't need italic or bold, they only need the right information.

With source code it's the same thing. Compilers (programs that turn code into other programs) are very strict with syntax. Some of them even care about where in the line a specific command is. Word processors mess up the position of text in lines far too much for compiler to like them. What you need is a clean view of what's in the source code or the configuration file to know that what you're writing is exactly what your system will get.

Some editors go even further: they became Integrated Development Environments (IDEs), that not only understand what you're typing (be it an Apache configuration or Java code) but can predict what you want to type, suggest modifications, or show your mistakes. They can color specific keywords, automatically place things in the right place, and so on.

But the most important is that all those colors and highlighting are done *only* within the display. Those fancy changes are **not** propagated to the text files, which are meant to be plain text. This is one particular useful feature that word processing programs can't do and is most essential to text editing.

WHY ARE MOST TEXT EDITORS COMMAND-LINE PROGRAMS?

In the beginning... was the command line (Neil Stephenson). Twenty years ago there weren't many graphical interfaces around and Unix was already a grown-up operating system running on a whole lot of very important computers. All configuration was already stored in text files because of the KISS principle (keep it short and simple). Unix made the most of KISS and plain text by helping programs work together on text files. Pipes (using the | character) are one powerful method of working together that you've seen in this book.

Nowadays, computers have thousands of times more power than those early ones, but keeping configuration in text files still gives a big advantage when the only connection you have to your server is through a 56-Kbit modem line and it's in a different country. Having to open a graphical interface might not be possible and if that's the only way you have to fix a problem, you're in big trouble.

Making graphical programs that deal with configuration was a big plus, as the average user can now change things without reading tons of documentation and isn't likely to break the system by inserting one wrong character to a point where it's irrecoverable, but providing text files and the command-line editor is fundamental to any operating system.

Although most text editors came from the command-line world, most also have a graphical interface today. Menus and buttons do help a lot when using Gvim or Emacs. GEdit and Kate (which are purely graphical) are short and simple, still providing the same basic functionality and the same important features for text editing.

SETTING A DEFAULT TEXT EDITOR

Because the terminal and command line are so tied in with the text editors, many commands open up a text editor for you. We saw one example `sudoedit`, in the "Useful Customizations" section. You can set the default editor though by setting either the EDITOR or the VISUAL environment variable. For instance:

```
$ export EDITOR=emacs
```

Put this in a startup file such as .lbashrc, and commands will use your chosen editor when they present a file for editing.

28. NANO

Nano is a simple editor. To open it and begin creating a new text file, type the following at the command line:

```
$ nano
```

Instead of a few lines of output, as you get with most commands in this book, the screen is taken over by the program as shown in Figure 1.

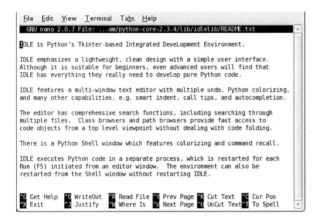

Figure 1. Opening screen for nano

The screen is no longer a place to execute commands; it has *become* a text editor. Since we typed nano by itself, we have the text editor open with a new (blank) file. We could also open an existing file by typing something like:

```
$ nano textfile.txt
```

The text from the file is now displayed within nano.

EXITING NANO

To exit nano, hold down the **Ctrl** key and press the **x** key (a combination we call **ctrl + x** in this book). If you have created some text but have not yet saved it, nano asks:

```
Save modified buffer (ANSWERING "No" WILL DESTROY CHANGES) ?
```

To save the changes, just type **y**. To abandon your changes, type **n**.

If you haven't typed anything into a new file, you have nothing to save so `nano` just exits without saying anything.

To save changes without exiting, press **ctrl + o**. `nano` asks you for the filename in which to save the text:

```
File Name to Write:
```

Type the name of the file, and press the **Enter** key. For instance:

```
File Name to Write: textfile.txt
```

EXPLORING FILES

You can move around the file and view different parts using the arrow keys. This is a very fast and responsive way to explore a file.

29. VI AND VIM

Vi is a very powerful command-line text editor. It's used for everything from quick fixes in configuration files to professional programming and even for writing large, complex documents like this book. It's popular on the one hand because it's fast and light-weight, and you can accomplish a lot with a few keystrokes. On the other hand it's also powerful: highly configurable, with many built-in functions.

Vim is an enhanced version of Vi, offering a lot of features that make life easier for both the novice and expert (Vim stands for "Vi IMproved"). On many modern systems, Vim is installed as the default version of Vi. So if you invoke the `vi` command you actually run Vim. This is usually not confusing, because everything in Vi works in Vim as well. We will look at Vim in this chapter, but if your system has Vi you can apply these techniques, just replace any reference to `vim` in the commands to `vi`.

The best feature about Vim/Vi is that it's shipped with virtually all GNU/Linux variants by default. Once you learn Vim, whenever you are, you can have the power of efficient editing.

The main drawback of Vim is, as for Emacs (another command line editor), the learning curve. The keyboard short-cuts a can be daunting to learn.

Fortunately, you can work around those drawbacks by using a graphical version of Vim (GVim) with all the buttons and menus for more graphical users. You can also try easy-Vim, with Notepad style editing.

These simplified versions of Vim reduce the learning curve a lot and expose less advanced users to the power of efficient editing, which in turn increases one's will to learn a more powerful editor.

BASIC COMMANDS

To open Vim and begin creating a new text file, get a command-line open and type:

```
$ vim
```

This presents you with a blank screen, or (if the program running is Vim) a screen of information looking something like this:

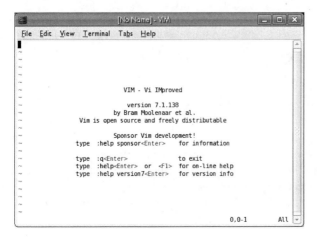

If you want to open an existing file, just specify it on the command line as an argument. For instance, the following opens a file called /etc/fstab:

```
$ vim /etc/fstab
```

This file already exists on most GNU/Linux systems, but if you open a non-existent file, you'll get a blank screen. The next section shows you how to insert text; when you're finished you can then save the file.

Inserting Text

Whether you have a blank screen or a file with text in it, you can add text by entering what's known as *edit mode*. Just press **i**. You should see this on the bottom of the screen:

```
-- INSERT --
```

Whenever this appears on the bottom of the screen, you are in edit mode. Whatever you type becomes part of the file. For instance, try entering "This is line 1." Then press the **Enter** key and enter "This is line 2". Here's what this fascinating contribution to literature looks like in Vim:

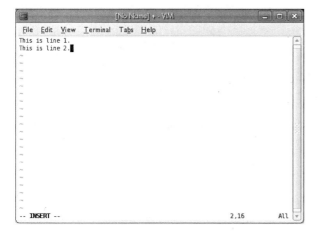

When you are finished inserting text, press the **Esc** (Escape) key to leave edit mode; that puts you in normal mode.

Only One Place At a Time: The Cursor

Vim, like every editor, keeps track of where you are and shows a cursor at that point, which may look like an underline or a box in a different color. In edit mode, you can backspace to remove characters. Vim also allows you to move around using arrow keys and edit the whole document freely. But normal Vi doesn't let you move around; it restricts you to adding text or backspacing to remove it.

In normal Vi, if you want to go back over what you edited, or move to another place in the file, you must press the **Esc** key, move to the place where you want to insert text, and enter edit mode again. This may seem cumbersome. But Vi provides so many alternate ways of moving around and adding text that you'll find, with some practice, that it's no barrier to productivity. As already mentioned, Vim lets you move around freely and edit the whole file when you're in edit mode--but you'll find yourself leaving edit mode often in order to make use of Vim's powerful commands.

Basic Movement Commands

To practice moving around in a file, you can press the **Esc** key to get out of edit mode. If you have only a small amount of text in the file, you may prefer to find another text file on your system that's larger, and open that. Remember that when you open a file you're in normal mode, not edit mode.

To move around use the arrow keys.

To jump to a specific line use the colon button followed by a line number. The following jumps to line 20:

```
:20
```

You can move quickly up or down a text file by pressing the **PgUp** and **PgDn** keys.

Search for text by pressing the slash key (/) and then typing the text you want to find:

```
/birthday party
```

You can simply repeat the **/** key to search for the next occurrence of the string. The search is case-sensitive. To search backward, press the question-mark key (**?**) instead of the slash key.

Saving and exiting

If you're in edit mode, you can save your changes by pressing **Esc** to go to normal mode, typing **:w** and pressing the **Enter** key. This saves your changes to the file you specified when you opened Vim.

Note: Vim, by default, does not save a backup of the original version of the file. Your **:w** command deletes the old contents forever. Vim can be configured to save backups, though.

If you opened Vim without specifying a file name, you receive an error message when you press **:w**:

```
E32: No file name
```

To fix this, specify **:w** with a filename:

```
:w mytestfile.txt
```

This must also be followed by the **Enter** key.

To exit Vim, press **:q**. If you have unsaved text, you receive an error message:

```
E37: No write since last change (add ! to override)
```

Like most word processors, Vim tries to warn you when you might make a mistake that costs you work. As the message suggests, you can abandon your text and exit by pressing **:q!**. Or use **:w** to save your changes and then enter **:q** again. You can combine writing and quitting through any of the following:

```
:wq (followed by Enter)
:x (followed by Enter)
ZZ
```

Practice!

30. EMACS

Emacs is a very powerful text editor. You can invoke Emacs by typing its name at the command line.

```
$ emacs
```

If you are using a typical graphics-based GNU/Linux distribution, this command opens a new window with Emacs running in that new window.

Emacs is an editor that is sufficiently powerful that many users open an Emacs session soon after turning their computer on and leave it open for the duration of their computing endeavor. If you plan to have Emacs running for an extended time, it is helpful to run Emacs in the background so that the command line becomes available for another command.

```
$ emacs &
```

You may occasionally want to run Emacs directly in the terminal window. Use the `-nw` (no window) option for this.

```
$ emacs -nw
```

You can load a file for editing at the time you start Emacs by giving the file name after the `emacs` command.

```
$ emacs filename
```

BASIC EDITING COMMANDS

Once Emacs is running, there are a number of basic editing commands you can use. In most of this book, outside of this Emacs chapter, we use a notation like **ctrl + x** to denote depressing the **Ctrl** (Control) key, then pressing the **x** key while **Ctrl** is depressed, then releasing both keys. In this Emacs chapter, we employ the notation used in the Emacs documentation, which abbreviates **ctrl + x** as **C-x**.

C-x C-f (load file into buffer)

The command **C-x C-f** (press the **Ctrl** key, press and release **x**, press and release **f**, release **Ctrl**) loads a file on disk into an Emacs *buffer* (an Emacs working area) for editing. You are prompted for the name of the file to load. You may then make changes to the buffer by typing and by using other Emacs commands. The buffer is not saved to a file on disk until you specifically request it with, for example, the **C-x C-s** command.

C-x C-s (save buffer to file)

The command **C-x C-s** saves the current Emacs buffer to disk as the currently named file. The name of the file is located on a bar at the bottom of the window.

C-x C-c (exit Emacs)

This command exits Emacs. If buffers remain that are unsaved, Emacs asks you whether you want to save them.

C-h t (start the Emacs tutorial)

The command **C-h t** (press the **Ctrl** key, press and release **h**, release **Ctrl**, press and release **t**) starts the Emacs tutorial. This takes you step-by-step through some basic Emacs commands.

C-h ? (general help)

This command offers a number of help options.

C-k (kill line)

The command **C-k** kills (deletes) the current line in the current buffer from the cursor to the end of the line.

C-y (yank back line)

This command "yanks back" the most recently killed line or set of lines and pastes it into the current cursor position.

OTHER EMACS FEATURES

Emacs has *major modes* for editing a variety of common and not-so-common file types, such as plain text, shell scripts, python language scripts, and so on. Each mode redefines the effect of hitting the **Tab** key, for example, to do the most appropriate thing for a particular file type. These modes start automatically for many types of files, based on the file extension or the first line in the file.

Emacs is extensible. You can program it to behave as you like, for example by using the inbuilt, easy to learn scripting language Emacs Lisp. See the Emacs documentation for more about this.

EMACS DOCUMENTATION

Emacs is well documented in free sources. Type `info emacs` at the command line (or **C-h r** from within Emacs) to read the full official documentation. There is also an abbreviated manual page (type `man emacs` at the command line). For beginners, the best way to start learning Emacs is the inbuilt interactive tutorial mentioned above.

31. KEDIT, KWRITE, & KATE

Although Kedit is part of the KDE software suite, which includes the KDE desktop environment, it does not require KDE to run. It is just as happy under Gnome. KDE has several built-in tools to help you edit text files (including scripts). The simplest of these is "KEdit", a basic text editor. You can start it from the KDE menu or from the command line, if you prefer. For example, you could run:

```
$ kedit /etc/profile &
```

You should see something like this.

```
# /etc/profile: system-wide .profile file for the Bourne shell (sh(1))
# and Bourne compatible shells (bash(1), ksh(1), ash(1), ...).

if [ "$PS1" ]; then
  if [ "$BASH" ]; then
    PS1='\u@\h:\w\$ '
    if [ -f /etc/bash.bashrc ]; then
       . /etc/bash.bashrc
    fi
  else
    if [ "`id -u`" -eq 0 ]; then
      PS1='# '
    else
      PS1='$ '
```

Using it is simple. You can move around the file with the arrow keys, Page Up (**PgUp**) and Page Down (**PgDn**) keys, or the mouse. Opening a new file is done from the **File->Open** menu, and you can spell-check your file with the **Tools->Spelling...** menu option.

At the bottom of the window is some useful information (if you don't see it, the **Settings->Show Statusbar** menu option brings it up). The line and column display shows the current position of the cursor. The "INS" means that you are in *insert mode*, and that if there is text to the right of the cursor, it is pushed over as you type. The opposite of this is "OVR", which stands for *overtype mode*, where text to the right is replaced by the newly typed text. You can switch between these with the **Insert** key on the keyboard.

If you make any changes to the current file, then "[modified]" appears in the title bar to remind you that you need to save changes before exiting.

KWRITE

While KEdit is useful, it is quite limited. KDE offers other options that are worth investigating. KWrite is very similar-looking, but offers useful additional features.

The most obvious advantage is *syntax highlighting*. For shell scripts, programs, and many other types of files, KWrite colors the text to make it easier to figure out what is going on. Here, comments are shown in gray, parameters are in green, built-in bash commands are shown in dark purple, and other shell commands in light purple. Generally KWrite tries to pick highlighting

148

based on what it guesses the type of file to be. If it guesses wrongly, or doesn't do highlighting at all, you can manually choose an option under **Tools->Highlighting**.

You might have also noticed the little minus symbols and lines in the left margin. This is part of what is known as *code folding*. KWrite tries to match up "if" statements with the corresponding "fi", "for" with "done", and so on. Clicking on the minus symbol collapses the block, which can be useful if you are reading through a script and are interested in viewing what comes before and after a block, but not what's inside it. There are many more helpful features that KWrite offers--take a look around the menu and see what things do!

KATE

Last up in this overview is Kate. It is essentially the same editor as KWrite. However, it offers additional tools that make working on a project, as opposed to a single file, easier.

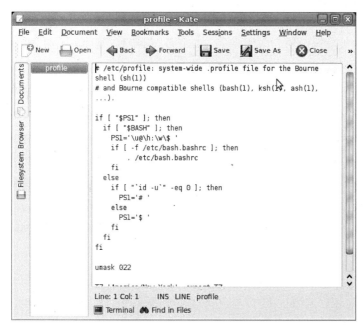

On the left side of the window are tabs that let you view the documents open in the current Kate session (KEdit and KWrite open multiple files in separate windows, while Kate can open them all in one), or navigate through your computer's filesystem to open a file. Kate also does syntax highlighting like KWrite, but also adds a "Terminal" tab at the bottom. Clicking on this tab opens and closes a mini-terminal where you can enter commands. In this case, if we wanted to see what "id -u" in the script does, and can simply type it in to the terminal to try it out.

For KDE users, KEdit, KWrite, and Kate offer three nice choices for editing text files. Chances are that all three came pre-installed on any system with KDE. Have fun trying them out!

32. GEDIT

Gedit, the default GUI editor if you use Gnome, also runs under KDE and other desktops. Most gNewSense and Ubuntu installations use Gnome by default. To start Gedit open a terminal and type

```
$ gedit &
```

You should see this:

This looks like most basic editors on any operating system. You can use Gedit through the GUI, and the commands are simple:

File->Open : Opens an existing file

File->New : Creates a new (blank) file

File->Save : Saves a file

ctrl + c : copy

ctrl + v : paste

That's all you really need to do. To add text just type!

LINE NUMBERS

Gedit tracks your cursor and displays the position at the bottom of the interface:

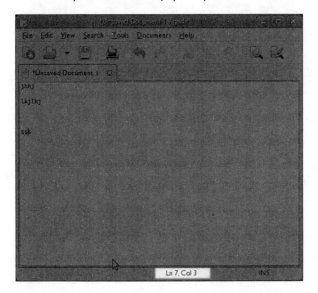

This can be handy information to know. If you keep track of the line numbers you can use these to jump quickly around the text file by using the "Go to Line" feature. This can be accessed via the interface (**Search -> Go to Line**) or via the shortcut **ctrl + i**.

SCRIPTING

33. SCRIPTING

If you have a collection of commands you'd like to run together, you can combine them in a script and run them all at once. You can also pass arguments to the script so that it can operate on different files or other input.

Like an actor reading a movie script, the computer runs each command in your shell script, without waiting for you to whisper the next line in its ear. A script is a handy way to:

- Save yourself typing on a group of commands you often run together.
- Remember complicated commands, so you don't have to look up, or risk forgetting, the particular syntax each time you use it.
- Use control structures, like loops and case statements, to allow your scripts to do complex jobs. Writing these structures into a script can make them more convenient to type and easier to read.

Let's say you often have collections of images (say, from a digital camera) that you would like to make thumbnails of. Instead of opening hundreds of images in your image editor, you choose to do the job quickly from the command line. And because you may need to do this same job in the future, you might write a script. This way, the job of making thumbnails takes you only two commands:

```
$ cd images/digital_camera/vacation_pictures_March_2009
$ make_thumbnails.sh
```

The second command, make_thumbnails.sh, is the script that does the job. It might look something like this:

```
#!/bin/bash
mkdir thumbnails
cp *.jpg thumbnails
cd thumbnails
mogrify -resize 400x300 *.jpg
```

The first line is optional. The initial hash mark (#) turns it into a comment that the shell ignores when executing the script. It's a useful line, though, because when you run the program, the line indicates that the /bin/bash program (in other words, the Bash shell) should be invoked to run the script. The line is also useful documentation for anyone who comes along and wonders what's in the file.

Each of the following lines is a command. We've seen three of them before: `mkdir`, `cp`, and `cd`. The last command, `mogrify`, is a program that can resize images (and do a lot of other things besides). Read its manual page to learn more about it.

MAKING SCRIPTS EXECUTABLE

To write a script like the one we've shown, open your favorite text editor and type in the commands you would like to run. You can put multiple commands on a single line so long as you put a semi-colon after each command so the shell knows a new command is starting.

Save the script. One common convention is to use the `.sh` extension -- for example, *make_thumbnails.sh*.

There is one more step before you can run the script: it has to be *executable*. Remember from the section on permissions that executability is one of the permissions a file can have, so you can make your script executable by granting the execute (**x**) permission. The following command allows any user to execute the script:

```
$ chmod +x make_thumbnails.sh
```

Because you're probably planning to use the script often, you'll find it worthwhile to check your PATH and add the script to one of the directories in it (for instance, */home/jdoe/bin* is an easy choice given the PATH shown here).

```
$ echo $PATH
/usr/bin:/usr/local/bin:/home/jdoe/bin
```

For simple testing, if you're in the directory that contains the script, you can run it like this:

```
$ ./make_thumbnails.sh
```

Why do you need the preceding *./* path? Because most users don't have the current directory in their PATH environment variables. You can add it, but some users consider that a security risk.

Finally, you can also execute a script, even without its execute bit set, by passing it as an argument to the command interpreter, thusly:

```
$ bash make_thumbnails.sh
```

MORE CONTROL

To provide the flexibility you want, the shell lets you make choices in a script and run things repeatedly on a variety of inputs. In that regard, the shell is actually a programming language, and a nice way to get used to using the powerful features a programming language provides. We'll get you started here and show you the kinds of control the shell provides through compound statements.

if

This statement was already introduced in the section on checking for errors, but we'll review it here. if is more or less what you'd expect, though its syntax is quite a bit different from its use in most other languages. It follows this form:

```
if [ test-condition ]
then
    do-something
else
    do-something-else
fi
```

You read that right: the block must be terminated with the keyword fi. (It's one of the things that makes using if fun.) The else portion is optional. Make sure to leave spaces around the opening and closing brackets; otherwise if reports a syntax error.

For example, if you need to check to see if you can read a file, you could write a chunk like this:

```
if [ -r /home/joe/secretdata.txt ]
then
    echo "You can read the file"
else
    echo "You can't read that file!"
fi
```

if accepts a wide variety of tests. You can put any set of commands as the test-condition, but most if statements use the tests provided by the square bracket syntax. These are actually just a synonym for a command named test. So the first line of the preceding example could just as well have been written as follows.

```
if test -r /home/joe/secretdata.txt
```

You can find out more about tests such as -r in the manual page for test. All the test operators can be used with square brackets, as we have.

Some useful test operators are:

-r	File is readable
-x	File is executable
-e	File exists
-d	File exists and is a directory

There are many, many more of them, and you can even test for multiple conditions at once. See the the manual page for test.

WHILE (AND UNTIL)

`while` is a loop control structure. It keeps cycling through until its test condition is no longer true. It takes the following form:

```
while  test-condition
do
    step1
    step2
    . . .
done
```

You can also create loops that run until they are interrupted by the user. For example, this is one way (though not necessarily the best one) to look at who is logged into your system once every 30 seconds:

```
while true
do
    who
    sleep 30
done
```

This is inelegant because the user has to press **Ctrl + c** or kill it in some other way. You can write a loop that ends when it encounters a condition by using the `break` command. For instance the following script uses the `read` command (quite useful in interactive scripts) to read a line of input from the user. We store the input in a variable named *userinput* and check it in the next line. The script uses another compound command we've already seen, `if`, within the `while` block, which allows us to decide whether to finish the `while` block. The `break` command ends the `while` block and continues with the rest of the script (not shown here). Notice that we use two tests through −o, which means "or". The user can enter **Q** in either lowercase or uppercase to quit.

```
while true
do
  echo "Enter input to process (enter Q to quit)"
  read userinput

  if [ $userinput == "q" -o $userinput == "Q" ]
  then
    break
  fi

  process input...

done
```

`until` works exactly the same way, except that the loop runs until the test condition becomes true.

CASE

`case` is a way for a script to respond to a generally small set of test conditions. It works similarly to case statements in other programming languages, though it has its own peculiar syntax, which is best illustrated through an example.

```
user=`whoami`  # puts the username of the user executing the script
               # into the $user variable.
case $user in
    joe)
        echo "Hello Joe. I know you'd like to know what time it is, so I'll show you
        date
        ;;
    amy)
        echo "Good day, Amy. Here's your todo list."
        cat /home/amy/amy-todo.txt
        ;;
    sam|tex)
        echo "Hi fella. Don't forget to watch the system load. The current system loa
        uptime
        ;;
    *)
        echo "Welcome, whoever else you are. Get to work now, please."
        ;;
esac
```

Each case must be followed by the) character, then a newline, then the list of steps to take, then a double semicolon (;;). The "*)" condition is a catchall, similar to the `default` keyword in some languages' `case` structures. If no other cases match, the shell executes this list of statements. Finally, the keyword `esac` ends the `case` statement. In the example shown, note the case that matches either the string "sam" or "tex".

FOR

`for` is a useful way of iterating through items in a list. It can be any list of strings, but it's particularly useful for iterating through a file list. The following example iterates through all of the files in the directory *myfiles* and creates a backup file for each one. (It would choke on any directories, but let's keep the example simple and not test for whether the file is a directory.)

```
for filename in myfiles/*
do
    cp $filename $filename.bak
done
```

As with any command that sets a variable, the first line of the `for` block sets the variable called *filename* without a dollar sign.

There's another variety of `for`, which is similar to the `for` construct used in other languages, but which is used less in shell scripting than it's used in other languages, partially because the syntax for incrementing and decrementing variables in the shell is not entirely straightforward.

34. MAINTAINABLE SCRIPTS

You are slowly delving into programming by the way of shell scripting. Now it's the best time to start to learn about how to be a good programmer. Since this book is just an introduction to the command line, we are only going to provide few but nevertheless very important hints centered around the idea of *maintainability*.

When programmers talk about maintainability they are talking about the ease with which a program can be modified, whether it's to correct defects, add new functionality, or improve its performance. Unmaintainable programs are very easy to spot: they lack structure, so functionality is spread all over the place. When you push *here* they break way over *there*, a real nightmare. In general, they are very hard to read. Consider for example this:

```
#!/bin/sh
identify `find ~/Photos/Vacation/2008 -name \*.jpg` | cut -d ' ' -f 3 | sort | uniq -c
```

use your favorite editor to save this file as *foo*, then:

```
$ chmod +x foo
$ ./foo
     11 2304x3072
     12 3072x2304
```

What that small monster does is find files that ends with ".jpg" in a certain directory, run identify on all of them, and report some kind of information that someone at some time must have thought very useful. If the programmer would only have added some hints as to what the programs does...

DON'T USE LONG LINES

The first thing you'll note is that our example of an unmaintainable program is one long line. There's really no need for that. What if the program looked like this instead:

```
#!/bin/sh
identify `find ~/Photos/Vacation/2008 -name \*.jpg` |
cut -d ' ' -f 3 |
sort |
uniq -c
```

It becomes a little bit easier to spot where each command begins and ends. It's still the same set of piped programs, only their presentation is different. You can break long lines at pipes and the functionality will be the same.

You can also split one command into several lines by using the \ character at the end of a line to join it with the next:

```
#!/bin/sh
echo This \
     is \
     really \
     one \
     long \
     command.
```

USE DESCRIPTIVE NAMES FOR YOUR SCRIPTS

The second thing you might have noticed is that the script is called "foo". It's short and convenient but it doesn't provide a clue as to what the program does. What about this:

```
$ mv foo list_image_sizes
```

Now the name helps the user understand what the script does. Much better, isn't it?

USE VARIABLES

One bothersome thing about that program is its use of backticks. Sure, it works, but it also has drawbacks. Perhaps the biggest one is the least evident one, too: remember that backticks substitute the output of the command they contain in the position where they appear. Some systems have a limit of the command line length they allow. In this particular case, if the specified directory has lots and lots of pictures, the command line can become extraordinarily long, producing an obscure error when you call the program. There are several methods that you can use to remedy this, but for the purpose of this explanation, let's try the following:

```
#!/bin/sh
find ~/Photos/Vacation/2008 -name \*.jpg |
while read image ; do identify $image ; done |
cut -d ' ' -f 3 |
sort |
uniq -c
```

Now find is running the same as before, but its output, the list of filenames, is piped into a while-loop. The condition for the loop is read image. read is a function that reads one line at a time, splits its input into fields and then assigns each field to a variable, *image* in this case. Now identify works on one image at a time.

Notice how introducing a variable makes the program a bit easier to read: it literally says that you wish to identify an image. Also note how the effect on future programmers wouldn't have been the same if the variable was called something like *door* or *cdrom*. Names are important!

But there's still something bothersome about the program: that directory name is glowing like a sore thumb. What if we change the program like this:

```
#!/bin/sh
START_DIRECTORY=~/Photos/Vacation/2008

find $START_DIRECTORY -name \*.jpg |
while read image ; do identify $image ; done |
cut -d ' ' -f 3 |
sort |
uniq -c
```

That's a little bit better: now you can edit your script and change the directory each time you wish to process a different one.

USE ARGUMENTS

That last bit didn't sound quite right, did it? After all, you don't edit ls each time you wish to list the contents of a different directory, do you? Let's make our program just as adaptable:

```
#!/bin/sh
START_DIRECTORY=$1

find $START_DIRECTORY -name \*.jpg |
while read image ; do identify $image ; done |
cut -d ' ' -f 3 |
sort |
uniq -c
```

The $1 variable is the first argument that you pass to your script ($0 is the name of the script you're running). Now you can call your script like this:

```
$ ./list_image_sizes ~/Photos/Vacation/2008
```

Or you can examine the 2007 pictures, if you wish:

```
$ ./list_image_sizes ~/Photos/Vacation/2007
```

KNOW WHERE YOU BEGIN

Consider what happens if you run the script like this:

```
$ ./list_image_sizes
```

Maybe that's what you want, but maybe it isn't. What happens is that $1 is empty, so $START_DIRECTORY is empty as well and in turn the first argument to find is also empty. That means that find will search your current working directory. You might wish to make that behavior explicit:

```
#!/bin/sh
if test -n "$1" ; then
    START_DIRECTORY=$1
else
    START_DIRECTORY=.
fi

find $START_DIRECTORY -name \*.jpg |
while read image ; do identify $image ; done |
cut -d ' ' -f 3 |
sort |
uniq -c
```

The program behaves exactly as before, with the only difference that in six months, when you come back and look at the program, you won't have to wonder why it's producing results even when you don't pass it a directory as argument.

LOOK BEFORE YOU LEAP

Speaking of which, what happens if you do pass an argument to the script, but that argument isn't a directory or better yet, it doesn't even exist? Try it.

Not pretty, ah?

What if we do this:

```
#!/bin/sh
if test -n "$1" ; then
    START_DIRECTORY=$1
else
    START_DIRECTORY=.
fi

if ! test -d $START_DIRECTORY ; then
    exit
fi

find $START_DIRECTORY -name \*.jpg |
while read image ; do identify $image ; done |
cut -d ' ' -f 3 |
sort |
uniq -c
```

That's better. Now the script won't even attempt to run if the argument it receives isn't a directory. It isn't very polite, though: *it silently exits* with no hint of what went wrong.

COMPLAIN IF YOU MUST

That's easily fixed:

```
#!/bin/sh
if test -n "$1" ; then
    START_DIRECTORY=$1
else
    START_DIRECTORY=.
fi

if ! test -d $START_DIRECTORY ; then
    echo \"$START_DIRECTORY\" is not a directory or it does not exist.  Stop.
    exit
fi

find $START_DIRECTORY -name \*.jpg |
while read image ; do identify $image ; done |
cut -d ' ' -f 3 |
sort |
uniq -c
```

MIND YOUR EXIT

The program now produces an error message if you don't pass it an existing directory as argument and it exits without further action. It would be nice if you let other programs that might eventually call your script know that there was an error condition. That is, it would be nice if your program exits with an error code. Something like this:

```
#!/bin/sh
if test -n "$1" ; then
    START_DIRECTORY=$1
else
    START_DIRECTORY=.
fi

if ! test -d $START_DIRECTORY ; then
    echo \"$START_DIRECTORY\" is not a directory or it does not exist.  Stop.
    exit 1
fi

find $START_DIRECTORY -name \*.jpg |
while read image ; do identify $image ; done |
cut -d ' ' -f 3 |
sort |
uniq -c
```

Now, if there's an error, your script's exit code is 1. If the program exits normally, the exit code is 0.

USE COMMENTS

Anything following a # symbol on a line will be ignored, allowing you to add notes about how your script works. For example:

```
#!/bin/sh
# This script reports the sizes of all the JPEG files found under the current
# directory (or the directory passed as an argument) and the number of photos
# of each size.

if test -n "$1" ; then
    START_DIRECTORY=$1
else
    START_DIRECTORY=.
fi

if ! test -d $START_DIRECTORY ; then
    echo \"$START_DIRECTORY\" is not a directory or it does not exist.   Stop.
    exit 1
fi

find $START_DIRECTORY -name \*.jpg |
while read image ; do identify $image ; done |
cut -d ' ' -f 3 |
sort |
uniq -c
```

Comments are good, but don't fall prey to writing too many comments. Try to construct your program so that the code itself is clear. The reason behind this is simple: next year, when *someone else* changes your script, that other person could well change the commands and forget about the comments, making the later misleading. Consider this:

```
# count up to three
for n in `seq 1 4` ; do echo $n ; done
```

Which one is it? Three or four? Evidently the program is counting up to four, but the comment says it's up to three. You could adopt the position that the program is right and the comment is wrong. But what if the person who wrote this meant to count to three and that's the reason why the comment is there? Let's try it like this:

```
# There are three little pigs
for n in `seq 1 3` ; do echo $n ; done
```

The comment documents the *reason* why the program is counting up to three: it is not describing what the program *does*, it's describing what the program *should do*. Let's consider a different approach:

```
TOTAL_PIGS=3
for pig in `seq 1 $TOTAL_PIGS` ; do echo $pig ; done
```

Same result, slightly different program. If you reformat your program, you can do without the comments (as a side note, the fancy word for the kinds of change we have been making is *refactoring*, but that goes outside the scope for this book).

AVOID MAGIC NUMBERS

In our current example, there's a *magic number*, a number that makes the program work, but no one knows why it has to be *that* number. It's magic!

```
...
cut -d ' ' -f 3 |
...
```

You have two choices: write a comment and document why it has to be "3" instead of "2" or "4" or introduce a variable that explains why by way of its name. Let's try the latter:

```
#!/bin/sh
# This script reports the sizes of all the JPEG files found under the current
# directory (or the directory passed as an argument) and the number of photos
# of each size.

if test -n "$1" ; then
    START_DIRECTORY=$1
else
    START_DIRECTORY=.
fi

if ! test -d $START_DIRECTORY ; then
    echo \"$START_DIRECTORY\" is not a directory or it does not exist.  Stop.
    exit 1
fi

IMAGE_SIZE_FIELD=3

find $START_DIRECTORY -name \*.jpg |
while read image ; do identify $image ; done |
cut -d ' ' -f $IMAGE_SIZE_FIELD |
sort |
uniq -c
```

It does improve things a little; at least now we know where the 3 comes from. If ImageMagick ever changes the output format, we can update the script accordingly.

DID IT WORK?

Last but not least, check the exit status of the commands you run. As it stands right now, in our example there's not much that can fail. So let's try one last example:

```
#!/bin/sh
# Copy all the HTML and image files present in the source directory to the
# specified destination directory.

SRC=$1
DST=$2

if test -z "$SRC" -o -z "$DST" ; then
    cat<<EOT
Usage:

    $0 source_directory destination_directory
EOT
    exit 1
fi

if ! test -d "$SRC" ; then
    echo \"$SRC\" is not a directory or it does not exist.  Stop.
    exit 1
fi

if test -e "$DST" ; then
    echo \"$DST\" already exists.  Stop.
    exit 1
fi

if ! mkdir -p "$DST" ; then
    echo Can\'t create destination directory \"$DST\".  Stop.
    exit 1
fi

# Obtain the absolute path for $DST
cd "$DST"
DST=`pwd`
cd -

cd "$SRC"

find ! -type d \( -name \*.html -o -name \*.jpg -o -name \*.png \) |
while read filename ; do
    dir=`dirname "$filename"`
    mkdir -p "$DST/$dir" && cp -a "$filename" "$DST/$filename"
    if test $? -ne 0 ; then
        echo Can\'t copy \"$filename\" to \"$DST/$filename\"
```

```
        echo Abort.
        exit 1
    fi
done
```

Note that this example makes use of many things you learned in this book. It does not try to be definitive; you can practice improving it!

The thing you should note now is how the program pays attention to the error conditions that the different programs might produce. For example, instead of just calling mkdir to check if a program worked, it does this:

```
if ! mkdir -p "$DST" ; then
    echo Can\'t create destination directory \"$DST\".  Stop.
    exit 1
fi
```

It calls mkdir as the condition for if. If mkdir encounters an error, it will exit with a non-zero status and the if clause will interpret that as a false condition. The "!" is a negation operator that inverts false to true (or vice versa. So the line as a whole basically says "Run the mkdir command, turn an error into a true value with the "!" operator, and take action if it's true that there's an error." In short, if mkdir encounters an error, the flow will enter the body of the if. This might happen, for example, if the user running the script doesn't have permissions to create the requested directory.

Note also the usage of "&&" to verify error conditions:

```
mkdir -p "$DST/$dir" && cp -a "$filename" "$DST/$filename"
```

If mkdir fails, cp won't be called. Furthermore, if either mkdir or cp fails, the exit status will be non-zero. That condition is checked in the next line:

```
if test $? -ne 0 ; then
```

Since this might indicate something going awfully wrong (e.g., is the disk full?), we had better give up and stop the program.

WRAPPING UP

Writing scripts is an art. You can become a better artist by looking at what others have done before you and doing a lot yourself. In other words: *read a lot of scripts and write a lot of scripts yourself.*

Happy hacking!

35. OTHER SCRIPTING LANGUAGES

The shell is a wonderful friend. If you have read the rest of the book up to this point, you may well be dizzy with the possibilities it presents. But the shell is still tremendously limited compared to many languages. We'll give you just a taste of other tools and languages you can explore.

Two classic tools, AWK and Sed, are commonly invoked from the shell. Each operates on input one line at a time. You can think of them as assembly lines on which workers load a file line by line. Each line is processed in order. These are classic examples of *filters*, an idea closely associated with GNU/Linux. Filters are strung together in pipes with the | character, with the output of each command becoming the input for the next.

The next section introduces regular expressions. They're a language all their own, but one where you can do a lot by learning a few simple features. They turn up in very similar forms all over: in text editors such as vi, in commands such as `grep`, in AWK and Sed, and in all the languages that follow.

Scripting languages were invented to make programming easy and allow people to create applications quickly. Unlike AWK and Sed, they usually run by themselves, not as part of pipes or other contexts where they just produce a line of output for each line of input. In contrast to the shell, these languages offer such advantages as:

- Versatile integer and floating-point arithmetic
- Objects, which help you keep data together with the functions that manipulate it
- Complex data structures that can store related data of many types

This book has short sections on the three most popular scripting languages in the free software world today: Perl, Python, and Ruby. You will encounter many tools and products that provide customization through those languages.

36. THE SED TEXT PROCESSOR

Sed (stream editor) is a utility that does transformations on a line-by-line basis. The commands you give it are run on each line of input in turn. It is useful both for processing files and in a pipe to process output from other programs, such as here:

```
$ wc -c * | sort -n | sed ...
```

BASIC SYNTAX AND SUBSTITUTION

A common use of Sed is to change words within a file. You may have used "Find and Replace" in GUI based editors. Sed can do this much more powerfully and faster:

```
$ sed "s/foo/bar/g" inputfile > outputfile
```

Let's break down this simple command. First we tell the shell to run sed. The processing we want to do is enclosed in double quotation marks; we'll come back to that in a moment. We then tell Sed the name of the *inputfile* and use standard shell redirection (>) to the name of our *outputfile*. You can specify multiple input files if you want; Sed processes them in order and creates a single stream of output from them.

The expression looks complex but is very simple once you learn to take it apart. The initial "s" means "substitute". This is followed by the text you want to find and the replacement text, with slashes (/) as separators. Thus, here we want to find "foo" in the inputfile and put "bar" in its places. Only the output file is affected; Sed never changes its input files.

Finally, the trailing "g" stands for "global", meaning to do this for the whole line. If you leave off the "g" and "foo" appears twice on the same line, only the first "foo" is changed to "bar".

```
$ cat testfile
this has foo then bar then foo then bar
this has bar then foo then bar then foo
$ sed "s/foo/bar/g" testfile > testchangedfile
$ cat testchangedfile
this has bar then bar then bar then bar
this has bar then bar then bar then bar
```

Now let's try that again without the /g on the command and see what happens.

```
$ cat testfile
this has foo then bar then foo then bar
this has bar then foo then bar then foo
$ sed "s/foo/bar/" testfile > testchangedfile
$ cat testchangedfile
this has bar then bar then foo then bar
this has bar then bar then bar then foo
```

Notice that without the "g", Sed performed the substitution only the first time it finds a match on each line.

This is all well and good, but what if you wanted to change the second occurrence of the word foo in our testfile? To specify a particular occurrence to change, just specify the number after the substitute commands.

```
$ sed "s/foo/bar/2" inputfile > outputfile
```

You can also combine this with the g flag (in some versions of Sed) to leave the first occurrence alone and change from the 2nd occurrence to the end of the line.

```
$ sed "s/foo/bar/2g" inputfile > outputfile
```

SED EXPRESSIONS EXPLAINED

Sed understands regular expressions, to which a chapter is devoted in this book. Here are some of the special characters you can use to match what you wish to substitute.

```
$ matches the end of a line
^ matches the start of a line
* matches zero or more occurrences of the previous character
[ ] any characters within the brackets will be matched
```

For example, you could change any instance of the words "cat", "can", and "car" to "dog" by using the following:

```
$ sed "s/ca[tnr]/dog/g" inputfile > outputfile
```

Remove any sequence of digits. The first [0-9] below ensures that at least one digit must be present to be matched. The second [0-9] may be missing or may be present any number of times, because it is followed by the * metacharacter. Finally, the digits are removed because there is nothing between the second and third slashes where you can put your replacement text.

```
$ sed "s/[0-9][0-9]*//g" inputfile > outputfile
```

Inside an expression, if the first character is a caret (^), Sed matches only if the text is at the start of the line.

176

```
$ echo dogs cats and dogs | sed "s/^dogs/doggy/"
doggy cats and dogs
```

A dollar sign at the end of a pattern expression tells Sed to match the text only if it is at the end of the line.

```
$ echo dogs cats and cats | sed "s/cats$/kitty/"
dogs cats and kitty
```

A line changes only if the matching string is where you require it to be; if the same text occurs elsewhere in the sentence it is not be modified.

DELETION

The "d" command deletes an entire line that contains a matching pattern. Unlike the "s" (substitute) command, the "d" goes after the pattern.

```
$ cat testfile
line with a cat
line with a dog
line with another cat
$ sed "/cat/d" testfile > newtestfile
$ cat newtestfile
line with a dog
```

The regular expression ^$ means "match a line that has nothing between the beginning and the end", in other words, a blank line. So you can remove all blank lines using the "d" command with that regular expression:

```
$ sed "/^$/d" inputfile > outputfile
```

CONTROLLING PRINTING

Suppose you want to print certain lines and suppress the rest. That is, instead of specifying which lines to delete using "d", you want specify which lines to keep.

This can be done with two features:

Specify the −n option, which means "do not print lines by default".

End the pattern with "p" to print the line matched by the pattern.

We'll show this with a file that contains names:

```
$ cat testfile
Mr. Jones
Mrs. Jones
Mrs. Lee                                                    Mr. Le
```

We've decided to standardize on "Ms" for women, so we want to change "Mrs." to "Ms". The pattern is:

```
s/Mrs\./Ms/
```

and to print only the lines we changed, enter:

```
$ sed -n "s/Mrs\./Ms/p" testfile
```

MULTIPLE PATTERNS

Sed can be passed more than one operation at a time. We can do this by specifying each pattern after an −e option.

```
$ echo Gnus eat grass | sed -e "s/Gnus/Penguins/" -e "s/grass/fish/"
Penguins eat fish.
```

CONTROLLING EDITS WITH PATTERNS

We can also be more specific about which lines a pattern gets applied to. By supplying a pattern before the operation, you restrict the operation to lines that have that pattern.

```
$ cat testfile
one: number
two: number
three: number
four: number
one: number
three: number
two: number
$ sed "/one/ s/number/1/" testfile > testchangedfile
$ cat testchangedfile
one 1
two: number
three: number
four: number
one: 1
three: number
two: number
```

The sed command in that example had two patterns. The first pattern, "one", simply controls which lines Sed changes. The second pattern replaces "number" with "1" on those lines.

This works with multiple patterns as well.

```
$ cat testfile
one: number
two: number
three: number
four: number
one: number
three: number
two: number
$ sed -e "/one/ s/number/1/" -e "/two/ s/number/2/" \
      -e "/three/ s/number/3/" -e "/four/ s/number/4/" \
      < testfile > testchangedfile
$ cat testchangedfile
one: 1
two: 2
three: 3
four: 4
one: 1
three: 3
two: 2
```

CONTROLLING EDITS WITH LINE NUMBERS

Instead of specifying patterns that can operate on any line, we can specify an exact line or range of lines to edit.

```
$ cat testfile
even number
odd number
odd number
even number
$ sed "2,3 s/number/1/" < testfile > testchangedfile
$ cat testchangedfile
even number
odd 1
odd 1
even number
```

The comma acts as the range separator, telling Sed to work only on lines two through three.

```
$ cat testfile
even number
odd number
odd number
$ sed -e "2,3 s/number/1/" -e "1 s/number/2/" < testfile > testchangedfile
$ cat testchangedfile
even 2
odd 1
odd 1
```

Sometimes you might not know exactly how long a file is, but you want to go from a specified line to the end of the file. You could use `wc` or the like and count the total lines, but you can also use a dollar sign ($) to represent the last line:

```
$ sed "25,$ s/number/1/" < testfile > testchangedfile
```

The $ in an address range is Sed's way of specifying, "all the way to the end of the file".

SCRIPTING SED COMMANDS

By using the `-f` argument to the `sed` command, you can feed Sed a list of commands to run. For example, if you put the following patterns in a file called *sedcommands*:

```
s/foo/bar/g
s/dog/cat/g
s/tree/houseg/
s/little/big/g
```

You can use this on a single file by entering the following:

```
$ sed -f sedcommands < inputfile > outputfile
```

Note that each command in the file must be on a separate line.

There is much more to Sed than can be written in this chapter. In fact, whole books have been written about Sed, and there are many excellent tutorials about Sed online.

37. AWK

AWK is a programming language designed for processing plain text data. It is named after its founders, Alfred **A**ho, Peter **W**einberger and Brian **K**ernighan. AWK is quite a small language and easy to learn, making it the ideal tool for quick and easy text processing. Its prime use is to extract data from table-like input.

Since programs written in AWK tend to be rather small, they are mostly entered directly on the command line. Of course, saving larger scripts as text files is also possible.

In the next paragraphs, we present present the basics of AWK through three simple examples. All of them will be run on the following text file (containing the five highest scores ever achieved in the video game Donkey Kong as of March 2009):

```
1050200 Billy Mitchell 2007
1049100 Steve Wiebe 2007
895400 Scott Kessler 2008
879200 Timothy Sczerby 2001
801700 Stephen Boyer 2007
```

The file is a table organized into *fields*. The first field of each row contains the respective score, the second and third fields contain the name of the person who has achieved it, and the fourth and last field of each row contains the year in which the score was set. You should copy and paste the text above into a text file and name it something like *highscores.txt* so that you can try out the following examples.

EXAMPLE 1

Let's say we want to print only those scores higher than 1,000,000 points. Also, we want only the first names of the persons who have achieved the scores. By using AWK, it's easy to extract this information:

```
$ awk '$1 > 1000000 { print $2, $1 }' highscores.txt
Billy 1050200
Steve 1049100
```

Try it out!

The little AWK program that we've just entered on the command line consists of two parts:

1. The part preceding the curly braces (*$1 > 1000000*) says "Do this for all lines where the value of field no. 1 is greater than 1,000,000."
2. The part inside the curly braces (*print $2, $1*) says "Print field no. 2, followed by field no. 1."

What the combined program says is: "For all lines, if the value of the first field is greater than 1,000,000, print the second field of the line followed by the first field of the line." (Note that AWK programs entered on the command line are usually enclosed in single quotation marks in order to prevent the shell from interpreting them.)

As we have seen in the previous example, the structure of an AWK statement is as follows:

pattern { *action* }

The expression *pattern* specifies a condition that has to be met for *action* to take effect. AWK programs consist of an arbitrary number of these statements. (The program we have discussed above contains only a single statement.) An AWK program basically does the following:

1. It reads its input (e.g. a file or a text stream from standard input) line by line.
2. For each line, AWK carries out all statements whose condition/pattern is met.

Simple, isn't it?

EXAMPLE 2

Let's look at another example:

```
$ awk '$4 == 2007 { print "Rank", NR, "-", $3 }' highscores.txt
Rank 1 - Mitchell
Rank 2 - Wiebe
Rank 5 - Boyer
```

The program, again consisting of a single statement, may be paraphrased like this: "For each line, if the value of field no. 4 equals 2007, print the word 'Rank', followed by the value of the variable 'NR', followed by a dash ('-'), followed by field no. 3."

So what this little program does is print the surnames of all high score holders having set their record in 2007 along with their respective ranks in the high score table.

How does AWK know which ranks the individual high score holders occupy? Since the table is sorted, the rank of each high score holder is equal to the row number of the entry. And AWK can access the number of each row by means of the built-in variable NR (**N**umber of **R**ow). AWK has quite a lot of useful built-in variables, which you can look up in its documentation.

EXAMPLE 3

The third and final example is a bit more complex than the other two, since it contains three AWK statements in total:

```
$ awk 'BEGIN {print "Together, the five best Donkey Kong players have achieved:"} {total
```

This will output the following:

```
Together, the five best Donkey Kong players have achieved:
4675600 points
```

Let's break up this program into its three parts/statements (which we have entered on a single command line):

First statement

pattern: BEGIN
action: print "Together, the five best Donkey Kong players have achieved:"

Second statement

pattern: none (= always execute *action*)
action: add the value of field no. I to the variable *total*

Third statement

pattern: END
action: print the value of the variable *total*, followed by the string "points"

OK, now let's look at what is new in this short AWK program.

First of all, the patterns BEGIN and END have a special meaning: the action following BEGIN is executed before any input is read and the action introduced by END is executed when AWK has finished reading the input.

In the second statement, we can observe that an AWK statement does not need a pattern, only *action* is obligatory. If a statement doesn't contain a pattern, the condition of the statement is always met and AWK executes the action for every single input line.

Finally, we have used our own variable for the first time, which we have called *total*. AWK variables do not need to be declared explicitly; you can introduce new ones by simply using them. In our example program, the value of the variable *total*, starting out at 0 (zero), is increased by the value of field no. I for each input line. The += operator means "add the math expression on the right to the variable on the left."

So after all input lines have been read, *total* contains the sum of all field 1 values, that is, the sum of all high scores. The END statement outputs the value of *total* followed by the string "points".

WHERE TO GO FROM HERE?

We have seen that AWK is a fun and easy to use little programming language that may be applied to a wide range of data extraction tasks. This short introduction to AWK can of course be little more than an appetizer. If you want to learn more, we recommend you have a look at GAWK, the GNU implementation of AWK. It is one of the most feature-rich implementations of the language, and comes with a comprehensive and easy to read manual (see http://www.gnu.org/software/gawk/manual/).

38. REGULAR EXPRESSIONS

When you're looking through files or trying to change text, your needs are often ambiguous or approximate. Typical searches include:

- Finding an indeterminate number of things, such as "one or more zeroes".
- Finding text that can have variants, such as "color" and "colour", or "gray" and "grey".
- Extracting parts of text that forms a pattern. For instance, suppose you have a list of email addresses such as <u>somebody@fsf.org</u> and <u>whoever@flossmanuals.net</u>, and you want to extract the parts after the @ sign (fsf.org and flossmanuals.net, respectively).

To search for such strings and (if you want) make replacements, a special language called *regular expressions* is invaluable. This section offers a quick introduction to regular expressions. The language can be intimidating at first--but it is not complicated, only terse. You have to use it a bit so that your brain gets used to picking the regular expressions apart.

The easiest way to learn and practice regular expressions is to use the simple filters provided with the shell, such as grep, Sed, and AWK. The grep command has popped up several times already in this book. In this section we'll use an "extended" version named egrep, because it provides more of the features people use frequently in regular expressions. Sed and AWK were introduced in previous sections; we'll use Sed a lot in this one.

By the end of this section, you'll understand grep, egrep, and Sed pretty well. You will then be able to move on and use regular expressions in other situations where they are even more powerful. Nearly every modern language, including the other scripting languages mentioned in this book (Perl, Python, and Ruby) offer regular expressions. Even databases offer some form of regular expressions.

The details of regular expressions vary from one tool to another, and even from one version of a tool to another version of the same tool. We'll show pretty common features, but they don't all work in every tool.

PLAIN TEXT

A regular expression doesn't have to be fancy. Up to now, the grep commands we've shown look for plain text:

```
$ cat color_file
Primary colors blue and red make the color magenta
Primary colors blue and green make the colour cyan
Primary colors red and green make the colour yellow
Black and white make grey
$ grep 'colour' color_file
Primary colors blue and green make the colour cyan
Primary colors red and green make the colour yellow
```

Because "colour" contains no metacharacters the shell would interpret, we don't need the single quotes, but we're using them to get into the habit. The egrep commands in this section will use lots of metacharacters.

INDETERMINATE QUANTITIES

One simple application of regular expressions is to search for "any number" of something, or a fuzzy amount such as "3 to 5" hyphens. Here are the metacharacters that support this. For the sake of simplicity, we'll show some in isolation and then use them in some tools.

Match zero or more of X	X*
Match one or more of X	X+
Match zero or one of X	X?
Match from 3 to 5 of X	X{3,5}

These look a lot like shell (globbing) metacharacters, but there are subtle differences. Focus on what they mean in regular expressions and remember that it is really a separate language from the shell metacharacters.

Now we can see how to find both "color" and "colour" in one search. We want either zero or 1 "u", so we specify:

```
$ egrep 'colou?r' color_file
Primary colors blue and red make the color magenta
Primary colors blue and green make the colour cyan
Primary colors red and green make the colour yellow
```

The asterisk (*) is one of the most common and useful metacharacters in regular expressions, but also one of the most confusing and misused. Suppose you wanted to remove zeros from a line. You might try to remove "any number of zeros" through an asterisk:

```
$ echo "There are 40006 items" | sed "s/0*/X/"
```

But the output is:

```
XThere are 40006 items
```

This happened because Sed replaces the first occurrence of the pattern you request. You requested "zero or more" and the first occurrence of that is the beginning of the line!

In this case, you want the plus sign (0+), but many versions of Sed don't support it. You can work around that with:

```
$ echo "There are 40006 items" | sed "s/00*/X/"
There are 4X6 items
```

If you put a single digit in the brackets, such as {3}, it means "match this number exactly". If you include the comma without a second digit, such as {3,}, it means "match any number of three or more."

INDETERMINATE MATCHES, CLASSES, AND RANGES

To match any character, just specify a dot or period (.). Thus, the following matches a slash followed by any single character and another slash:

```
$ egrep '/./' file
```

The dot is commonly combined with one of the fuzzy quantifiers in the previous section. So the following matches any number of characters (but there has to be at least one) between slashes:

```
$ egrep '/.+/' file
```

The following is the same except that it also finds lines with two slashes in a row (//):

```
$ egrep '/.*/' file
```

A period is a common character in text, so you often want a dot to mean a dot--not to have its special metacharacter meaning. Whenever you need to search for a character that your tools considers a metacharacter, precede it with a backslash:

```
$ egrep '\.' file
```

That command finds just a dot. Because the backslash causes the dot character to escape being treated as a metacharacter, we speak of *escaping* characters through a backslash.

If you find yourself searching for strings that contain punctuation and you don't want any of the punctuation treated as a metacharacter, it can be tiresome and difficult to escape each character. Consider using fgrep (which stands for "fixed grep") for these strings instead of grep or egrep. The fgrep command looks for exactly what you pass, and doesn't treat anything as a metacharacter. You still have to use single quotes so the shell doesn't treat anything as a metacharacter.

Square brackets let you specify combinations of characters. For instance, to search for both "gray" and "grey" you specify:

```
$ egrep "gr[ae]y" color_file
Black and white make grey
```

To match the letters that are commonly used as vowels in English, write:

```
[aeiouy]
```

The order of characters never matters inside the brackets. We can find lines without vowels by submitting the regular expression to egrep. We'll start with a rather garbled file name *letter_file*:

```
This is readable text.
Ths s grbg txt.
This is more readable text.
aaaai
```

Note that the second line contains no vowels, whereas the last line contains only vowels. First we'll search for a vowel:

```
$ grep '[eauoi]' letter_file
This is readable text.
This is more readable text.
aaaai
```

The line without vowels failed to match.

Now let's look for non-vowel characters. That means not only consonants, but punctuation and spaces. We can *invert* the character class by putting a caret (^) at the front. In a character class (and nowhere else) the caret means "everything except the following". We'll do that here with five vowels (allowing the "y" to be matched because it can also be a consonant):

```
$ grep '[^eauoi]' letter_file
This is readable text.
Ths s grbg txt.
This is more readable text.
```

This time only the last line was left out, because it had vowels and nothing else.

A character class can also contains ranges, which you indicate by a hyphen separating two characters. Instead of [0123] you can specify [0-3]. People often use the following combinations:

Any digit	[0-9]
Any lowercase letter	[a-z]
Any uppercase letter	[A-Z]
Any letter	[a-zA-Z]

As the last example in the table shows, you can combine ranges inside the brackets. You can even combine ranges with other characters, such as the following combination of letters with common punctuation:

```
[a-zA-Z.,!?]
```

We didn't have to escape the dot in this example because it isn't treated as a metacharacter inside the square brackets.

Note that a character class, no matter how large, always matches a single character. If you want it to match a lot of characters, use one of the quantifiers from the previous section:

```
$ egrep '\([a-zA-Z.,!?]+\)' file
```

This matches parentheses that enclose any number of the characters in the character set. We had to escape the parentheses because they are metacharacters--very special ones, it turns out. We'll look at that next.

GROUPS

Parentheses allow you to manipulate multiple characters at once. Remember that character classes in square brackets always match a single character, even though that single character can be many different things. In contrast, groups can match a sequence. For instance, suppose you want to match quantities of a thousand, a million, a billion, a trillion, etc. You want to match:

1,000

1,000,000

1,000,000,000

etc.

You can do that by putting the string ",000" in a group, enclosing it in parentheses. Now anything you apply to it--such as the + character--applies to the whole group:

```
$ egrep '1(,000)+' file
```

But parentheses do even more. They store what they match, which is called *capturing* it. Then you can refer to it later.

This is a subtle and possibly confusing feature. Let's show it by looking at a file that repeats some sequences of characters:

```
This bell is a tam-tam.
This sentence doesn't appear in the egrep-generated output.
I want it quick-quick.
```

The first line contains the word "tam", a hyphen, and then "tam" again. The third line contains "quick", a hyphen, and then "quick" again. These lines don't actually have strings in common, except for the hyphen (which appears in the second line too, so searching for it doesn't distinguish the first and third lines from the second). What the first and third lines share is a pattern: a word followed by a hyphen and itself. So we can grab those two lines by capturing a word and repeating it (the file is named *doubles*):

```
$ egrep ' ([a-z]+)-\1' doubles
This bell is a tam-tam.
I want it quick-quick.
```

Puzzled? The regular expression, broken into pieces, is:

(	Start a group
[a-z]+	Any number (one or more) of letters
)	Close the group
-	Hyphen (a simple match)
\1	Repeat the group captured earlier

The \1 is a special syntax recognized by tools that allow parentheses to capture text. In the first line of the files, it matches "tam" because that's what [a-z]+ matched. In the third line, it matches "quick" because that's what [a-z]+ matched. It says, "whatever you found, I want it again."

To extract the second part of an email address, such as "fsf.org" from "someone@fsf.org", use a regular expression such as:

```
([a-z._]+)@([a-z._]+)
```

In this case, \1 matches the part before the @ sign, while \2 matches the part after the @. So extract \2 to get "fsf.org".

ALTERNATION

We saw that a character class matches only one character at a time. If you have two or more sequences that can appear in the same place, you specify them through *alternation*. This involves separating them with a vertical bar (|). Thus, the following finds an instance of "FSF" or "Free Software Foundation":

```
FSF|Free Software Foundation
```

You can put as many alternatives as you want in alternation:

```
gnu.org|FSF|Free Software Foundation
```

Because the alternatives are usually embedded in a larger regular expression, you generally need to put them in parentheses to mark where they start and end:

```
The (FSF|Free Software Foundation)
```

ANCHORING

If you want to match something when it occurs at the beginning of the line, but nowhere else, preface the regular expression with a caret (^). Thus, you can use the following to catch lines that begin with a lowercase letter:

```
^[a-z]
```

This use of the caret has nothing to do with the caret that we saw before inside of square brackets. A caret means "beginning of line" when it's the first character of a regular expression, but only in that position.

Similarly, you can match something at the end of a line by adding a dollar sign ($) to the end of the regular expression:

```
[0-9]$
```

In the phrase "I added 3 and 5 to make 8", the previous regular expression will match the 8 because it's at the end of the line.

When you're searching for lines that match a regular expression exactly (no extra text at the start or end), use both anchors. For instance, if you want to make sure a line consists only of digits, enter:

```
^[0-9]+$
```

The [0-9]+ part specifies "one or more digits", and the ^ and $ ensure that the regular expression takes up the whole line.

We wanted to take you just far enough to get a sense of what regular expressions can do for you. There are many, many more features, but some of them are useful only in programming languages. As we warned before, different tools support different features, so you have to read the documentation for egrep, Sed, or any other tool or language to find out what works there.

When you're testing regular expressions, you can try lots of online or stand-alone tools (some offered gratis and some for sale) that help debug problems such as mismatched brackets and parentheses. Such tools can help you learn the more complex features and make complex regular expressions easier to write.

39. PERL

Perl is a programming language that can be used to perform tasks that would be difficult or cumbersome on the command line. Perl is included by default with most GNU/Linux distributions. Usually, one invokes Perl by using a text editor to write a file and then passing it to the `perl` program.

Perl scripts can be named anything but conventionally end with ".pl". You can use any text editor to create this file -- Emacs, Vim, Gedit, or whatever your favorite is. A script could look like this:

```
my $a = 1 + 2;
print $a,"\n";
```

In this example, we create a variable (by using *my*) which is called *$a* (the dollar sign is Perl's way of denoting a variable), which stores the result of "1 + 2". It then uses the *print* function to print the result, which should be 3. The comma concatenates two or more strings together. In this case a newline is appended to the end of the printed string. All statements in Perl are terminated with a semicolon, even if they are on separate lines. If we save this file as *first.pl*, we can run it from the command line.

```
$ perl first.pl
3
```

The Perl program printed out "3", just like we expected. Of course, we can use Perl to do more useful things. For example, we can look at all the files in the current directory.

```
my $filename;
opendir DH, "." or die "Could not open directory!";
while( $filename = readdir(DH) ){
  print $filename,"\n";
}
```

```
$ perl first.pl
perl-script.perl
other-script.perl
document.odt
photo.png
```

Here we use the *opendir* function to open a directory for reading. "DH", will be our directory handle, how we refer to the open directory for reading. A directory handle is not declared like a variable, just created at the invocation of the *opendir* function. We pass the directory name as a string (enclosed in double quotes); the single dot refers to the current directory. The *or* and *die* statements tell Perl to terminate execution if the directory cannot be opened. The final string tells Perl what to print as an error message.

Inside the *while* loop, the *readdir* function takes our directory handle and returns the next *filename* in the directory, storing it in the default variable "$_".

Let's try doing something with these files -- here's a way to find all of the ".pl" files in a directory.

```
opendir DH, "." or die "Could not open directory!";
while( $_ = readdir(DH) ){
  print $_,"\n" if /.pl$/;
}
```

Above we use a Perl shorthand to compress the print and evaluation into one line since both *print* and *if* take the default variable "$_" as their argument if one is not specified. The "/.pl/" operator says: match any word that ends with ".pl". Below is a simpler but wordier way to pick out the all of the files with ".txt" in them.

```
my $filename;
opendir DH, "." or die "Could not open directory!";
while( $filename = readdir(DH) ){
  if ($filename =~ /.txt$/){
    print $filename,"\n";
  }
}
```

Perl uses braces ({ }) to group statements in branching and loop constructs, such as *if* and *while*. The "=~" operator tells *if*, yes, when ".txt" appears at the end of the variable or string.

We can also use command line code in Perl by using the *system* function. For example, if we wanted to delete all of the ".txt" files, we could use.

```
my $dir = "./";
system("rm $dir*.txt");
```

Above, *system* passes its argument to a shell, which executes it exactly as it would if we typed it in. Now if we look for any files ending in, ".txt" we won't find any.

```
system("ls *.txt");
```

MORE INFORMATION ABOUT PERL

The Perl web site at http://www.perl.org contains an impressive amount of information and documentation about the Perl language.

40. PYTHON

Python is a programming language that can be used to perform tasks that would be difficult or cumbersome on the command line. Python is included by default with most GNU/Linux distributions. Just like the command line, you can either use Python by typing commands individually, or you can create a script file. If you want to type commands individually, start the Python interpreter by typing `python`.

```
$ python
>>> 10 + 10
20
```

To exit an interactive Python session, type **Ctrl + d**.

To write a multi-line script in Python that you can run from outside of the Python interactive console, you first must create a file and then save it with a ".py" extension at the end of the file name. You can use any text editor to create this file -- Emacs, Vim, Gedit, or whatever your favorite is. A script could look like this:

```
a = 1 + 2
print a
```

In this example, we create a variable, *a*, which stores the result of "1 + 2". It then uses the *print* command to print out the result, which should be 3. If we save this file as *first.py*, we can run it from the command line.

```
$ python first.py
3
```

The Python program printed out "3", just like we expected. Of course, we can use Python to do more useful things. For example, we can look at all the files in the current directory.

```
$ python
>>> import os
>>> os.listdir('.')
['notes.txt', 'readme.txt', 'first.py']
```

Here we import the standard library "os", which has operating system-like functions in it. We call the *listdir* function to return a list of names of files in the current directory. We pass the directory name as a string (enclosed in single quotes); the single dot refers to the current directory.

Let's try doing something with these files -- here's a way to find all of the ".py" files in a directory.

```
>>> files = os.listdir('.')
>>> files
['notes.txt', 'readme.txt', 'first.py']
>>> [file for file in files if '.py' in file]
['first.py']
```

Above we use a powerful construction called a *list comprehension* to produce a new list by transforming and filtering a list. Below is a simpler but wordier way to pick out the all of the files with ".txt" in them.

```
>>> for file in files:
...      if '.txt' in file:
...          print file
...
notes.txt
readme.txt
```

The indentation is required in Python. Indentation tells the Python interpreter what to include in the *for* loop and what to include in the *if* statement. Also, a you must press an additional **Enter** at the last set of three dots to tell the Python interpreter that you're done.

We can also use command line code in Python by passing it to the *os.system* function. For example, if we wanted to delete all of the ".txt" files, we could use.

```
>>> for file in files:
...      if '.txt' in file:
...          cmd = 'rm ' + file
...          os.system(cmd)
...
```

Above, we construct a shell command *cmd* as a Python string by concatenating (using the "+" operator) the strings "rm " and the filename, then pass it to the *os.system* function. Now we can check to see that the files have been deleted.

```
>>> os.system('ls')
first.py
```

MORE INFORMATION ABOUT PYTHON

The Python web site at http://www.python.org contains an impressive amount of information and documentation about the Python language. If you are just getting started with programming, the book "How to Think Like a Computer Scientist" by Jeffrey Elkner, Allen B. Downey and Chris Meyers at http://openbookproject.net/thinkCSpy/index.xhtml is a good place to start.

41. RUBY

Ruby is a programming language that can be used to perform tasks that would be difficult or cumbersome on the command line. To get started with Ruby, you need to install it. Usually, there is a program on your computer such as "Add/Remove Programs" or "Package Manager" which allows you to easily install Ruby. You can also go to http://www.ruby-lang.org, where you can find downloads for Ruby as well as more information on the language.

Just like the command line, you can either use Ruby by typing commands in individually, or you can create a script file. If you want to type commands in individually, install the "irb" program and use the `irb` command at the command line:

```
$ irb
> 10 + 10
=> 20
> exit
$
```

As you can see, you can use Ruby to do basic mathematics. An important note about Ruby is that instead of printing a value only when you use *echo* (which is *puts* in Ruby) , Ruby will print out the result of whatever command you enter -- this is what the "=>" means. When you enter the "10 + 10" command, the result is "20". Also, remember that you can use *exit* to get out of the `irb` program.

To write a multi-line script in Ruby, you create a file and save it with a ".rb" at the end. You can use any text editor to create this file -- Emacs, Vim, Gedit, or whatever your favorite is. A script could look like this:

```
a = 1 + 2
puts a
```

In this example, we create a variable, *a*, which stores the result of "1 + 2". It then uses the *puts* command to print out the result, which should be 3. If we save this file as *ruby.rb*, we can run it from the command line:

```
$ ruby ruby.rb
3
```

The Ruby program printed out "3", just like we expected. Of course, we can use Ruby to do more useful things. For example, we can look at all the files in a directory:

```
$ irb
> Dir.entries('my-directory')
=> ["ruby-script.rb", "other-script.rb", "document.odt", "photo.png"]
```

We used the *Dir.entries* method to look at the files in *my-directory*. You probably noticed that we pass parameters differently in Ruby. Instead of separating them with spaces, we surround them in parenthesis. We also need to enclose all words in quotes - not just ones that have special characters in them.

Let's try doing something with these files -- here's a way to find all of the ".rb" files in a directory:

```
> files = Dir.entries('my-directory')
=> ["ruby-script.rb", "other-script.rb", "document.odt", "photo.png"]
> for file in files
> puts file if file.include?('.rb')
> end
ruby-script.rb
other-script.rb
```

First, we used the *for* command to loop through each of the files. We then get to work with each file. The next line says that we want to print out the file if it includes the text ".rb". Finally, we end the *for* loop.

We can also use command line code in Ruby by enclosing it in backticks. For example, if we wanted to delete all of the ".rb" files, we could use:

```
> files = Dir.entries('my-directory')
=> ["ruby-script.rb", "other-script.rb", "document.odt", "photo.png"]
> for file in files
> `rm #{file}` if file.include?('.rb')
> end
```

Notice how we enclosed the `rm` command in backticks. We also used #{} to enclose the Ruby variable, so it is put in to the command properly instead of the literal string "file".

LEARNING MORE ABOUT RUBY

If you want to learn more about Ruby, http://www.ruby-lang.org is the homepage for Ruby, and http://www.ruby-doc.org is a great place to find tutorials and documentation.

APPENDICES

42. GLOSSARY

&

(ampersand) Execute command in background.

>

Redirect standard output.

>>

Append standard output.

<

Redirect standard input.

|

Pipe, connecting the standard output of the preceding program with the standard input of the following program. You can break long program lines after pipe symbols without changing their effect.

.

(dot) In a file path, this refers to the current directory. Before a shell script name, this means to execute the script as if typed into the current shell, rather than starting a new shell and executing the command in its environment.

..

(double dot) Parent of the current directory. The parent of the root directory / is itself.

~

(tilde) Home directory.

/

(slash) By itself or at the beginning of a path, the root directory; in a path, the directory separator. Thus in /usr/bin, it serves both functions.

(backslash) At the end of a line, continues a long command on the next line. Before a special character, escapes that character, so that commands can deal with filenames that contain special characters. This allows users to search for text containing special characters, for example by using "*" to search for "*".

# #

(hash) Comment.

*

(splat) In file globbing, wildcard to match any string. In regular expressions, wildcard to match any number of occurrences of the previous element.

?

Wildcard to match any character.

^

(caret) Wildcard to match the beginning of a line.

!

(bang) On the command line, execute the last command that begins with the following characters. Thus !mv says to run the last mv command. This function has modifiers to allow editing the last command before running it, to search for strings within commands, to run commands by number, to run the most recent command and to run different commands with the same arguments.

In logical expressions, such as those inside if and while statements, negate the result of the following expression. For example,

```
$ if ! mkdir -p "$DST" ; then exit 1
```

attempts to create a new directory, and exits if the directory cannot be created.

{}

In a command following the -exec option of the find command, this is replaced by the name of a file that was found, so that the given command is applied to every found file.

` `

(backtick backtick) Execute command inline, and replace it with the result.

$( )

Execute command inline, and replace it with the result.

[\$( )]

Execute a command within a prompt.

$

(dollar) In a command, indicates that the value of the following environment variable should be used, not the name. For example, `echo $USER`. In regular expressions, a wildcard to match the end of a line. Dollar is also usually the last character in a bash prompt.

#!

(hashbang) Marks the beginning of an executable script. Follow with the program to execute this file, as in `#!/bin/bash`.

ABSOLUTE PATH

A file path starting from the root directory, such as `/usr/share/doc`. Contrast with **relative path**.

ALIAS

The alias command gives a name to a command string. Aliases can be made permanent by putting them in a bash startup script such as `~/.profile`.

APT-GET

Advanced Packaging Tool, a user interface command for managing and installing gNewSense and Debian packages.

APTITUDE

Terminal-mode package manager for Debian-style packages.

ARCHIVE

A file, usually compressed, containing multiple files.

ARGUMENT

An input value required for a command to process. Also called "parameter". Contrast with **option**.

ASH

A smaller version of the Bourne shell (sh). The ash shell is a clone of Berkeley's Bourne shell (sh). Ash supports all of the standard sh shell commands, but is considerably smaller than sh. The ash shell lacks some Bourne shell features (for example, command-line histories), but it uses a lot less memory.

ASPELL

GNU Aspell is a free software spell checker designed to eventually replace Ispell. It can either be used as a library or as an independent spell checker.

AWK

A scripting language for data extraction and analysis from structured text files.

AUTO COMPLETION

When the shell can determine that there is only one file starting with the latest text on the command line, pressing **Tab** will fill in the rest of the name. If there are several matches, the shell will fill in the part of the names (if any) that is unique, and let the user continue from there.

BACKGROUND

By adding an ampersand, "&", at the end of a command you tell the shell to run the program in the background, without terminal input, and to give you a prompt so that you can continue to give commands.

BASH

The GNU Bourne Again shell, the default shell in the GNU/Linux operating system. Bash is an sh-compatible shell that incorporates useful features from the Korn shell (ksh) and C shell (csh). It is intended to conform to the IEEE POSIX P1003.2/ISO 9945.2 Shell and Tools standard. It offers functional improvements over sh for both programming and interactive use. Most sh scripts can be run by Bash without modification.

BUG

Program behavior other than expected or desired.

BUG REPORT

Usually an e-mail or an entry in a bug database asking for help with a specific bug. Good bug reports state what software was used (Linux distribution and version, application name and version), what the user tried to do and what was the expected result, what happened instead, and what the user tried in order to fix it. It is particularly helpful to explain how to reproduce the problem, if it is repeatable. Log files of the incident should be attached.

BUILTIN

A command executed by the shell itself, not by calling a separate program. The bash command

```
$ man builtins
```

gives details on builtins for bash itself.

CHARACTER SET

A collection of abstract characters, independent of the shapes in any particular font, with a numbering and one or more encodings. The ASCII character set maps to the numbers 0-127, encoded in seven bits of an eight-bit byte. ISO-8859-1 and related character sets have the range 0-255, and are encoded in 8 bits. Unicode maps to the numbers 0-1,114,111 (17 16-bit code pages of 65,536 code points each), and has several encodings, of which the most commonly seen is the variable-length UTF-8.

CLOBBER

Overwrite a file with new data. A common result of forgetting to append standard output with ">>" and instead writing a new file with ">".

COMMAND

Executable file or shell builtin.

COMMAND COMPLETION

In bash and other shells typing part of a command or file name that is on the path or in the current directory, and then pressing **Tab**, often fills in the rest of the name. If not, pressing **Tab** again gives a list of names beginning with the characters so far typed.

COREUTILS

The GNU Core Utilities are the basic file, shell and text manipulation utilities of the GNU operating system. These are the core utilities which are expected to exist on every operating system.

CRON JOB

A command to be executed automatically on a schedule set with the `cron` command or one of its variants, such as `anacron`.

DEFAULT

In many commands, the value preset for a particular option if the command line does not specify something different. The user can specify a default value for unset environment variables, for example,

```
$ cat "${VARIABLE_FILE_NAME:=/home/user/file}"
```

DEPENDENCY

Software required to run a particular piece of software. This can include other applications, library files, fonts, images, and other data.

DIRECTORY

A special kind of file that lists specific information on the files it contains, including owner, group, and permissions.

DIRECTORY STACK

A place to store recently used directory paths for easy retrieval with the commands `pushd` and `popd`. The command `dirs` displays the directory stack.

EMACS

GNU Emacs text editor, originally short for Editing Macros, now jocularly Escape, Meta, Alt, Control, Shift, from its pervasive reliance on key combinations. You can be sure that emacs can do it, you just need to find out how.

ENVIRONMENT VARIABLE

A string value assigned to a name in the environment of the current shell.

ESCAPE

A character that changes the interpretation of a character or sequence of characters that follow it. This is the original use of the Escape character. For example, in a text search the character "*" matches a wide range of text, while the string "*" matches only an asterisk.

EXIT STATUS

A value returned by a command to the shell, useful in scripting for deciding what to do next.

FILE

Utility for determining file types.

FILESYSTEM

The basic directory layout for a GNU/Linux system.

FILTER

Command-line program that reads standard input and writes standard output so that it is suitable for use in a pipeline, where each command performs a specific transformation on the data.

FINDUTILS

The GNU versions of find utilities. find, locate, updatedb and xargs.

FLOSS

Free/Libre Open Source Software, licensed so as to guarantee the essential freedoms of software users to source code and reuse. A combination of Free Software and Open Source Software, with Libre added in to emphasize that software freedom is essentially a matter of rights, not price.

FOLDER

The name used in GUIs for directories.

FONTCONFIG

Font configuration and customization library.

FTP

The standard File Transfer Protocol client.

FUNCTION

In bash, the function builtin allows the user to create functions on the fly with the syntax

```
$ function name() {body}
```

GAWK

The GNU version of the awk text processing utility. gawk is a program that you can use to select particular records in a file and perform operations upon them.

GEDIT

A simple and easy text editor for GNOME. It is UTF-8 compatible, provides tools for editing source code and can be extended using plugins.

GLOBBING

Referring to a group of files with an abbreviation, such as "*" for all of the files in a directory.

GNOME

A desktop, set of libraries, and application suite for X.

GNU

Recursive acronym for GNU's Not Unix. It is the Free Software Foundation project to create a freely-licensed replacement for the proprietary Unix operating system.

GNU/LINUX

Operating system combining the Linux kernel with GNU software tools.

GRAPHICAL USER INTERFACE (GUI)

User interface offering windows, icons, mouse control, multiple fonts, and so on.

GREP

The GNU versions of grep pattern matching utilities. Grep searches one or more input files for lines containing a match to a specified pattern.

GROUP

To simplify security, Unix systems organize users into groups, and assign a group owner as well as an individual owner to every file. In this way, system operators, for example, can be given control over certain system resources all at once, or everybody working on a project can gain access to all project files by joining the project group. Each user has a group with the same name for that user's files.

GZIP

The GNU data compression application. gzip.org

HISTORY

Record of previously executed commands that can be recalled and executed again with the up arrow key.

INTLTOOL

Utility for internationalizing various kinds of data files.

KERNEL

The Linux kernel, core of the GNU/Linux operating system. kernel.org

KERNEL-UTILS

Kernel and Hardware related utilities.

LESS

A text file browser similar to `more`, but better as it can move back and forth through the file.

LOCALE

Values of a set of environment variables that store information on the user's language, country, and character encoding, and options for date and time formatting, money, measurements, and other such information. Also the name of the command to display all of these environment variables.

LOG

A file, often in the `/var/log` directory, that contains notes made by running programs about their progress and about any problems they encounter. Vital information whenever something goes wrong.

LSOF

A utility which lists open files on a GNU/Linux system.

LYNX

A text-based Web browser. lynx.browser.org

MAKE

An essential program for installing much unpackaged source code software. The developers can write down all of the complex information about how to configure, compile, and install their work in make files that you usually won't have to read. Just check the README or INSTALL files that come with the source code to see whether it uses this system, or has different instructions. Another program with similar functions is jhbuild.

MAN

A set of documentation tools: man, apropos and whatis.

MC

The Midnight Commander, a user-friendly text console file manager and visual shell.

MORE

A utility for displaying text files one screenful at a time. See also *less*.

OPENSSH

The OpenSSH implementation of SSH protocol versions I and 2.

OPTION

A value specified to a command using the form `--option` (long option) or `-o` (short option). Contrast with **argument**, which is a required input.

PACKAGE MANAGER

Software to install, remove, and otherwise manage applications as packaged by a particular distribution, particularly making sure that dependencies and compatibilities between software components are observed. The two main varieties are Red Hat/Yellow Dog `yum` and Debian `apt-get`.

PARAMETER

Argument.

PASSWD

The passwd utility for setting/changing passwords using PAM. netadmintools.com

PATH

Environment variable specifying where the current shell should look for command files.

PERL

Practical Extraction and Report Language, or jocularly, Pathologically Eclectic Rubbish Lister. Perl is a dynamic programming language particularly suitable for text processing and manipulation.

PIPE

A connection between two commands, so that the standard output of the first becomes the input of the second. Indicated with the character "|".

PLAIN TEXT

A message or file represented as a sequence of characters in a specific character encoding, with no extra formatting information. Contrast with **rich text**. HTML files are plain text, but contain markup tags so that they represent rich text.

PROCESS

A running program. Each process has a process ID, a number that you can use to identify the process in a command.

PROMPT

The text string displayed by a shell when waiting for command input.

RECURSIVE COMMAND EXECUTION

With the -r or -R options, many commands will act on the current directory and any subdirectories. Check command documentation to determine the precise syntax.

REDIRECTION

Sending a file or standard output from a command to standard input of a command, or sending standard output or error output of a command to standard input of another command, or to a file.

REGULAR EXPRESSION

A string such as "*.png" that defines a pattern for matching text or filenames using special characters to indicate which alternatives to include.

RELATIVE PATH

A file path starting from the current directory, such as docs or ../Pictures. Contrast with **absolute path**.

RICH TEXT

Text with formatting, including fonts, multiple type sizes, positioning, color, and much more. HTML and word processing files are forms of rich text. Contrast with **plain text**.

ROOT

1. root user, or superuser, a required account with permission to do anything on a GNU/Linux system.
2. The starting point of the directory tree, written "/". All other directories are specified by paths from this root directory.

SCRIPT

An executable text file.

SED

A GNU stream text editor.

SHELL

A command interpreter such as sh or bash.

STACK

A way to keep track of tasks and other information so that the last item saved (pushed) on the stack is the first item retrieved (popped) from the top of the stack. An example is the bash history stack.

STANDARD INPUT, STANDARD OUTPUT, AND STANDARD ERROR

Communication channels provided to every running command. If not otherwise specified at the command line, they connect to the user's terminal, but they can be redirected to files or through pipes to other programs.

STRING

A string is a sequence of characters in a particular character set. Examples in ASCII include the sentence "Hello, World", the URL "http://www.flossmanuals.net/", and the text message "No such file or directory." Unicode strings can include any combination of languages, such as "Japan (□□) and Korea (□□□□)".

SUDO

A command to allow specified users and groups to run specified programs with superuser privileges. The file /etc/sudoers contains the specifications. The command sudoedit is provided for editing this file. It checks whether the edited file is in the correct format.

SUPERUSER

The root account, which has all permissions.

SYNTAX HIGHLIGHTING

Displaying the text of various elements of a program, such as function names, variable names, strings, and keywords, in distinctive colors appropriate to the programming language (bash, Perl, Python, etc.) or markup format (HTML, XML, etc.) used. The colors are not stored with the file, but computed by the text editor when loading a file and during editing.

TELNET

The client program for the telnet remote login protocol.

TERMINAL

Originally, a printing terminal such as a Teletype, or a video terminal. Now a virtual terminal in a text or graphics window. In all cases, a device or program for typing input and displaying output.

TIME

A GNU utility for monitoring a program's use of system resources.

UNICODE

The universal character set, meant to replace the jumble of more than a hundred other character set standards for 30 modern writing systems and dozens of others.

UNZIP

A utility for unpacking zip archives.

UTC

Coordinated Universal Time, or Temps Universel Coordonné, which has replaced Greenwich Mean Time as the world standard. The abbreviation UTC is a compromise between the English and French names.

VI

Visual editor, a powerful terminal-mode editor.

VIM

The VIM editor, an extension of vi.

WGET

A utility for retrieving files using the HTTP or FTP protocols.

WHICH

Displays where a particular program in your path is located.

WILDCARD

A character that can match more than one string in file globbing or regular expression matching.

X

The standard windowing system for GNU/Linux.

YUM

Yellowdog Update Manager, a package manager used in Red Hat and related GNU/Linux distributions that use RPM packages.

ZIP

A file compression and packaging utility compatible with PKZIP.

43. COMMAND QUICK SURVEY

In each of the command examples in this chapter, the dollar sign ($) at the beginning of the line is a minimal GNU/Linux command prompt. (Your default prompt is usually more complex.)

The rest of the line is the command, with options and arguments. We use the following conventions.

- Lines that do not begin with "$ " are responses from the command execution.
- The "|" character pipes the output of any command to another command.
- The ">" character redirects the output of any command to a file.
- To append output to a file, use ">>".
- Many commands have no output. They succeed or fail silently, but return an error code that a script can use to decide what to do next.
- The ";" character separates commands on the same line. They are executed in sequence, starting at the left.
- The "&" character at the end of a command line says to execute the command in the background, and give the user prompt for the next command immediately.
- The "\" character at the end of a command line says that the command continues on the next line. Although the examples given in this manual are generally quite short, there are cases where commands span five or six lines in script files.
- In 'some text with spaces ' and "more text with spaces", the single and double quotes indicate that the text inside is one argument, including the trailing space in the first example. Without them, the shell would interpret each word as a separate argument and discard whitespace.
- Backticks "```" mark commands to be executed. The result is substituted for the command.
- A number of commands have an option, usually written $-r$ or $-R$, for applying the command to every file in every subdirectory of the location where the command starts its work. Since these options can be and are used for other functions, you should check the documentation on any command where you want to use this capability.

A change that many people make is to put this command in their their startup file, .bashrc or .profile.

```
$ PATH=$PATH:.
```

This adds the current directory (.) to the path, so that you can execute your own private commands from one of your directories by changing to the directory and typing the command name. Without this, you have to type `./command` to execute a command in the current directory. Some people consider this a security risk. Some prefer

```
$ PATH=~/bin:$PATH
```

so that they can execute scripts in a directory of their choosing that they own, and those scripts will take precedence over others of the same name. However they will not accidentally execute scripts randomly anywhere in the filesystem that they happen to be.

LS

`ls` is the command to list filenames.

It can have options (Flags) added after the command with a minus sign "-".
Arguments (parameters) can also be added.

$ ls	ordinary file listing
$ ls | less	pipe listing to less, which displays it a page at a time
$ ls > filelist	redirect listing to file named "filelist"
$ ls -l	long file listing (file sizes, change times,..)
$ ls -a	include filenames starting with ".", normally not listed
$ ls -l -a	applies both the above options
$ ls -la	equivalent to the previous command
$ ls *.fort	list files called "ANYTHING.fort"
$ ls -lat *.fort	the t means list them in time order, not alphabetically

These examples show the main points of all GNU/Linux commands. They are short, they take options, they take parameters, you can user several options together, you can chain commands together with pipes, you can redirect the output of a command to a file.

To list all files under a particular directory, use the -R option.

```
$ ls -R
photos1 photos2 photos3

./photos1:
centraal_station.jpg     nieuwe_kerk.jpg

./photos2:
ica.jpeg                 sanders_theater.jpeg

./photos3:
bayeux_cathedral.jpeg    rouen_cathedral.jpeg     travel.odt
```

The "R" stands for "recursive." Note that the recursive option is uppercase -R in the ls command (-r is used to reverse the ordering the directory contents), but can be either uppercase or lowercase in the rm command.

MAN, INFO

Now that you know the basics of shell commands, use these often; you can learn almost anything you need from the ample (if terse) documentation they provide.

You can get a summary of almost any GNU/Linux command with the man command or the more recently developed info command. If the man command doesn't work, it is probably because your shell can't find the manual pages. This requires you to set the variable MANPATH to the correct directories. To find the directories that contain manual pages, try the following command. It means "print directories that have the name *man*":

```
$ find / -type d -name man -print
```

Manual pages follow a fairly rigid format. They start with a command synopsis, then list all the options and arguments to the command. Other sections that may be present include a short description; examples, overview, defaults, exit status, environment variables, and known bugs.

Info presents similar material, but often with more detail, and split into several pages with navigation links.

APROPOS

The apropos command tells you about man files that contain any keyword you specify, including man pages about topics other than commands. You would have a hard time guessing the names of some of these topics without help from apropos.

```
$ apropos -a samba password
smbpasswd (5)          - The Samba encrypted password file
```

PWD

GNU/Linux has directories to help you organize your files. pwd tells you your "current working directory" or CWD. In directory specifications, "." stands for the current directory, and ".." for the parent directory. Paths starting with "/" are absolute, with no dependence on the current directory. Paths starting without a "/" are relative to the current directory.

An example directory name would be /home/allen/handy/scripts. The full name starts with a slash "/" and directory names are separated by slashes. This differs from Windows, which uses the backslash "\", and Macintosh, which uses ":".

```
$ pwd
/home/myname
```

CD

Changes your CWD.

$ cd	change to your "home directory"
$ cd ..	takes you to the parent directory, for example from /usr/lib to /usr
$ cd Docs	change to documents directory in current directory, if there is one (uses relative path)
$ cd /usr/lib	takes you to the dir "/usr/lib" from anywhere (uses absolute path)
$ cd /	The root directory - there are none above this.

Your "home directory" is the one you log in to. It is defined in the file /etc/passwd (unless some special network system is in use, in which case it is found in the output from ypcat passwd).

MKDIR

Make a directory.

```
$ mkdir mydirectory
```

RMDIR

Remove a directory.

```
$ rmdir mydirectory
```

TOUCH

If a file exists, this updates its modification date and time. If there is no such file, it is created with nothing in it.

```
$ touch newfile
```

RM

This command removes files (and directories).

By default, you get no second chance, and once files are gone they are irretrievable. A nasty joke sometimes played on Newbies is to suggest "rm -r *" as the remedy for whatever problem they have. Don't try this unless you want to install a new operating system from scratch anyway, and you have a complete, current backup.

$ rm filename(s)	
$ rm -r filename(s)	Remove directories and all their contents.
$ rm -i filename(s)	Prompt for a y/n choice before each file (recommended!)
$ rm -f filename(s)	Do not complain if the file does not exist. Also overrides the -i flag.

LN

Make hard links or symbolic (aka "soft") links to files. Both hard links and soft links are references to other files. If you don't know what an "inode" is, stick with using soft links. (Even if you *do* know what an inode is, chances are good that you will use soft links the vast majority of the time).

A soft link is a special type of file that serves as an alias to another file (or directory) -- same basic concept as "desktop shortcuts" in Windows, where you have a shortcut icon on your desktop that points to a program, file, or folder that is located elsewhere on your computer. The file or directory that the link points to is called the "target" of the link.

When using ln, remember to include the -s option to choose soft type of link, and put the path to the target *before* the destination path for the new link.

To create a soft link named "linkname" pointing to a target named "file":

```
$ ln -s file linkname
```

To create links in the current directory (also known as ".") that point to files in ending in ".so" located in the ../*lib* directory, giving the soft links the same names as the original files:

```
$ ln -s ../lib/*.so .
```

CP

This command copies files.

$ cp file1 file2	Copies file1 over file2, if it exists. Creates file2 if it did not exist.
$ cp /etc /home/allen	Copies /etc to /home/allen/etc
$ cp -r mydir mynewdir	With the -r flag, copies directories too

MV

This moves and renames files and directories.

$ mv file2 file3	Renames a file or directory
$ mv /home/allen/etc /tmp	Moves a file or directory

WHOAMI

This tells you your id name, for example, "allen"

So you can type

```
$ grep `whoami` /etc/passwd
```

to see your home directory and some other things.

```
allen:!:5037:1:P. Allan:/u/allen:/bin/csh
```

The grep command is used to search for strings in text files.

The backticks `` cause execution of the command inside. The result, in this case "allen", is substituted in the outer command, exactly as if the user had typed grep allen /etc/passwd.

The ! in the second field tells the computer that the encrypted password is held in another file. This makes it a bit harder for dishonest people to get hold of your password.

PASSWD

This should be one of the first commands you use when given a new id. It sets your password, and can do a few other things too. You will be prompted for the old password (if any) and will be asked for the new password twice. (length = 8 characters)

EXAMPLE

```
$ passwd
Changing password for "allen"
allen's Old password:
allen's New password:
Enter the new password again:
$
```

There are restrictions on what you can choose, but they are in /etc/security and so not readable!

Good passwords are hard to guess, but also hard to remember. It is best to use all 8 characters and include at least one of [a-z], [A-Z] and [0-9]. There are programs around that guess many passwords, so it is unwise to use any passwords based on names, real words, the user id, the hostname, or other guessable strings.

EXIT

This stops your session or just one window (if in a window). exit detects jobs that are paused (by **Ctrl + z** for instance) because they would die if you used exit. Type exit a second time if you are happy with that. Running background jobs continue.

When using a graphical interface, a menu accessed with the mouse can be used to end your whole session. Window managers are not built into GNU/Linux, and vary greatly.

PS

Get a list of running processes. By default, ps lists only processes in the current shell. To get a list of all of your processes, use ps -e.

```
$ ps
  PID TTY          TIME CMD
29477 pts/0    00:00:00 bash
29811 pts/0    00:00:00 ps
```

KILL

Terminate a running process without allowing it to complete. Particularly useful if a program has gotten into an infinite loop in which it does not receive or process keyboard input.

```
$ kill 29477
```

Kills the process with Process ID 29477. In the `ps` example above, this would be the current shell.

CHOWN

Every file has an owner and a group, as you can see with the `ls` command. You should have a group named the same as your account. The Change Owner command, `chown`, lets you set these ownership attributes for files that you have the right to write.

You can give an entire group permission to read, write, or execute files with one command. If you want to keep files private, set the group to consist only of you, and use `chmod` (below) to restrict access by others. The following assumes that, when your user account was created, a group just for you with the same name was created. This is true on many modern systems, but not on all.

```
$ chown user:user myfile
```

If you have imported some directories that came in with the wrong ownership, you can change them all with one command. Just `cd` to the top directory, and execute this command, with the appropriate user and group names. The `-R` option tells `chown` to go through every subdirectory, and the * wildcard tells it to change ownership of every file and directory it finds there.

```
$ chown -R user:group *
```

CHMOD

Every file and directory has a "filemode" consisting of a list of attributes.

You can see this with `ls -l`.

```
$ cd ; ls -la
```

The ";" separates two commands on the same line.

That shows you the modes of the files in your home directory.

Included in the list should be two entries called "." and "..", which refer to your current directory and its parent.

You will see a set of characters showing the file's permissions, followed by the owner (your ID, probably, for all except ..) and the group (perhaps "staff"), a file size, the time and date of the last change to the file, and the name. The listing will resemble the following:

```
total 312
drwxr-x---  16 allen    staff      1024 Oct 21 14:07 .
drwxr-xr-x  21 sys      sys         512 Oct 13 16:25 ..
-rwxr-----   1 allen    staff       896 Oct 20 14:44 .cshrc
drwx------   2 allen    staff       512 Oct  6 08:51 .elm
-rw-r--r--   1 allen    staff        59 Oct 17 13:59 .exrc
-rwxr-----   1 allen    staff       461 Oct 17 12:18 .login
. . .
```

A "d" in column 1 means the entry is a directory. A "-" means it is a file.

See the manual page for `ls`, under the `-l` option, for other possible file types.

There are 9 other characters in 3 sets of 3.

Columns 2-4 are for the file's OWNER. (named later on the line, "allen" in this case)

Columns 5-7 are for the file's GROUP. (named later on the line, "staff" in this case)

Columns 8-10 are for everyone else, except the superuser who always has all permissions.

- "r" grants read permission.
- "w" grants write permission.
- "x" grants execute permission. For a directory, this means search permission.
- "-" denies the permission in that location.

See `man ls` under the `-l` flag for other possible modes. Notice that write permission on a directory allows you to remove files from that directory *even if you do not own the files.*

```
chmod 640     file1   # sets file1 to -rw-r-----
chmod 755     file2   # sets file2 to -rwxr-xr-x
chmod go=     file3   # sets file3 to -???-------   (removes group & other)
chmod -R go-w $HOME   # GOOD SAFE COMMAND: only you can write in your home dir
```

MORE, LESS, PG, CAT

These commands allow you to look at text files.

```
$ more .bashrc
$ less /etc/motd
$ cat /etc/fstab
```

The more, less, and pg commands allow you to page through a file and search for strings. The less command ironically has somewhat more options than more.

When in a more, less, or pg session type the **h** key to see what commands you can use.

The cat command displays the entire file, so it is good only for files that fit on one or two screens. The original purpose of cat (catenate) is to join text files together, but it is extremely useful for displaying short individual files.

```
$ cat file1 file2 > file3
```

GREP

Find and display lines in one or more files. The earliest version, grep, is named after a common command form in an early line editor, Global Regular Expression Print, which searched through an entire file for text patterns and displayed the matching lines. Regular expressions, described in another section of this manual, provide methods for specifying text patterns. Options permit searching groups of files, including all subdirectories of the starting point. One of the most common uses of grep is to find lines in configuration and log files specific to one user or one program.

```
$ grep `whoami` /etc/passwd
```

looks for the result of the whoami command in the password file, returning the user's account information, though with the password obscured.

DF

Disk Free. Show sizes of storage media, space used, and space available. Shows sizes in blocks (a size that varies from one filesystem to another) by default, so use the −h option to get sizes in "human-readable" form: K for thousands of bytes, M for millions of bytes, and G for billions of bytes.

```
$ df -h
Filesystem              Size   Used  Avail  Use%  Mounted on
/dev/sda1               143G    41G    96G   30%  /
tmpfs                   941M      0   941M    0%  /lib/init/rw
varrun                  941M   380K   941M    1%  /var/run
varlock                 941M      0   941M    0%  /var/lock
udev                    941M   2.7M   939M    1%  /dev
tmpfs                   941M   844K   940M    1%  /dev/shm
lrm                     941M   2.4M   939M    1%  /lib/modules/2.6.27-11-generic/volatile
```

ECHO

Repeat after me, with substitutions if desired. Literal echoes are quite useful in scripts.

```
$ echo "Hello, world."
Hello, world.
$ echo $PATH
/home/myname/bin:/usr/local/sbin:/usr/local/bin:/usr/sbin:/usr/bin:/sbin:/bin:/usr/games
```

FILE

This makes an attempt to recognize files, classifying them as English Text or executable or data.
type

```
$ file * | less
```

to see some examples.

XLF:	ascii text
doc:	directory
handy:	directory
groceries:	ascii text
.Xauthority:	data or International Language text
.cshrc:	commands text
.exrc:	English text

DIFF

Differences between two text files. It also tells you whether two binary files differ.

```
$ diff .profile~ .profile
 23a22
> scim -d &
```

This says that line 23 was added (in this case, to support typing in multiple languages and character sets), and shows the new contents of the line.

WC

WORD COUNTS, PLUS LINE AND CHARACTER COUNTS.

```
$ wc .login
6       7     461 .login
```

This *.login* file has 6 lines, 7 words, and 461 characters.

The program counts any string of printing characters between whitespace as a word, which can give strange results by human standards.

FIND

To list all files or directories named *core* under the current working directory:

```
$ find . -name core -ls
```

To remove all files named *core* under the current working directory (useful because programs create these files when they terminate through a programming error, but the files are of little value to you unless you possess and can read the source code):

```
$ find . -name core -exec rm {} \;
```

To list all files or directories named *"something*.core" under the current working directory:

```
$ find . -name '*.core' -ls
```

To name all directories called *man* under /usr:

```
$ find /usr -name man -type d -print
```

The next 2 examples are useful for removing temporary files you no longer want.

```
$ find /tmp /var/tmp -mtime +3 -type f -user allen -exec rm {} \;
$ find /var/preserve -mtime +8 -type f -user allen -exec rm {} \;
```

The next example names files and directories which *either* have changed in the last 2 days, *or* have execute permission for the owner.

```
$ find . \( -mtime -2  -o -perm -100 \) -print
```

Checking what has changed during the last few days is a great way to find out why your computer isn't working any more!

FTP

Upload and download files using File Transfer Protocol. Use:

```
$ ftp hostname
```

to connect to the ftp archive at *hostname*. The FTP protocol specifies how to log in, navigate directories on the archive, upload and download files or groups of files, and much more. This summary gives you enough commands to navigate an archive and to download files (and upload them, if you have permission).

When you connect to a repository, you will see a > prompt where you can enter commands.

```
> binary
```

Set to binary mode, which passes every byte of the file unchanged. This should be the first command you give, unless you are absolutely certain that you will download only text files.

```
> ascii
```

Set to text mode, which converts line ends. This is the default when FTP starts. It is safe for text in ASCII, other 8-bit encodings, and Unicode UTF-8. **Do not use for programs, images, music, and other binary files.**

```
> dir
```

List files in the current directory on the remote host.

```
> cd directory-name
```

Change directory.

```
> cdup
```

Change to the parent directory of the current directory on the remote host.

```
> get remote-file [local-file]
```

Download a file and optionally rename it.

```
> put local-file [remote-file]
```

Upload a file and optionally rename it.

```
> bye
```

End the `ftp` session.

WGET

Download files from the Internet reliably, even over unreliable connections. If the connection goes down during a download, `wget` can resume from where it left off when the connection comes back up.

```
$ wget URL
```

will download the file at the URL to the current directory, using the same name. There are, as you would expect, numerous options.

TAR

The Tape Archive utility creates a single tar file containing the contents of one or more files, or extracts files from a tar file. Although originally designed to produce combinations of files for backup to tape, it is still the standard utility for packing together files so you can move them around as a unit. As an option, the files can be compressed in a tgz file.

```
$ tar -cf foo.tar foo/
```

Store contents of folder *foo* in *foo.tar*. The `-c` option creates a tar file. The `-f` option says to use the filename given. Without `-f`, the result would go to standard output. You can use this form in a pipeline to use a different compression method, such as bzip2, described below.

```
$ tar -cvfz foo.tgz foo/
```

Store compressed contents of folder *foo* in *foo.tgz*, and give moderately verbose output on the console as each file is processed. More verbose output is available with the `vv` option.

```
$ tar -xf foo.tar
```

Extract *foo.tar* in the current directory.

```
$ tar -xzf foo.tgz
```

Extract gzipped *foo.tgz*. The tgz extension is an abbreviation of the formerly common .tar.gz, used when combining files and compressing the result required piping the output of tar to the input of gzip.

GZIP, GUNZIP, ZCAT, BZIP2, BUNZIP2, BZCAT

The zip and bzip2 file compression algorithms are among the most popular of many ways to make files smaller (originally for transmission over slow modem connections), so that the inverse algorithms restore the full original files unchanged. Although the bzip2 method achieves better compression than zip, it also requires more processor time. For each one, we'll show a command for compression, decompression, and combining multiple files into one. The tar utility can use gzip compression.

```
$ gzip file
```

or

```
$ bzip2 file
```

compresses a file into an archive. The name of the archive file is the same as the original file, with the extension ".gz" or ".bz2" added.

```
$ gunzip file.gz
```

Decompress the *file.gz* archive to the original file.

The `gunzip` command is equivalent to `gzip -d`, where the `-d` option stands for "decompress". Similarly, `bunzip2` is equivalent to `bzip2 -d`.

The `zcat` utility is equivalent to `gunzip -c`, where the `-c` option says to write the uncompressed results into a single file. This is frequently useful when a directory contains a number of compressed text files. For example,

```
$ zcat *.txt.gz
```

Combining the output into one file makes it easier to search. You could pipe the output of this command to `grep`, for example. Similarly, `bzcat` is equivalent to `bzip2 -c`.

LYNX

The World-Wide Web is so widely used that some people think it is the entire Internet, but originally the Web was designed to use only text, and there are several text browsers for it still in use. Lynx (a pun on "links") remains popular among those who spend more time at the command line or inside Emacs than in a GUI.

A text browser can simply ignore any material marked with HTML tags that refer to graphical content, or can display the ALT text that is often supplied with images, both for the sake of text browsers and for the blind and visually impaired.

```
$ lynx url
```

starts Lynx. If you specify a URL, Lynx will start with that page. Otherwise, it will go to its current default home page, which you can set to point wherever you like.

The following table gives you enough commands to use Lynx, but there are many more.

?	Help
K	List commands
+	Scroll down one screen
-	Scroll up one screen
□	Next link
□	Previous link
Return or □	Follow link
□	Back
a	Add current link as bookmark
d	Download current link to file
g	Go to URL
o	Set options
p	Print
s	Search
v	View bookmarks
q	Quit Lynx.

MIDNIGHT COMMANDER

The Midnight Commander (mc) is based on concepts from the Norton Commander for PCDOS, which provides a two-pane file browser, and puts many DOS commands on function keys and menus. For GNU/Linux, of course, mc offers GNU/Linux commands in a text terminal window. The command to start it is, of course, mc.

```
$ mc
```

The screen shot below shows a typical display in Midnight Commnander. You will have a different directory structure and different files.

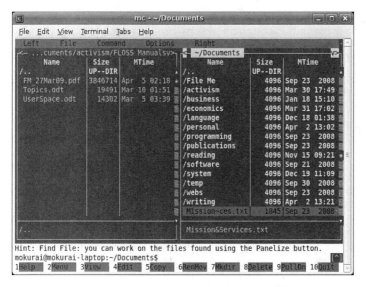

You can navigate using either the mouse or the keyboard. **Tab** moves you to the other panel. The **Insert** key highlights files and directories for actions such as copy, rename, move, and delete, which you can see on the function key buttons, or for various commands on the pull-down menus.

The Left and Right menus let you change views to give different information, to enter a regular expression that determines which files to display, or to sort in a different order, among other things. You can invoke FTP from either of these menus, and use Midnight Commander's file commands to upload and download files. The File menu includes commands such as chmod and chown, with a visual dialog for selecting options and on-screen help, as shown in the screenshot below.

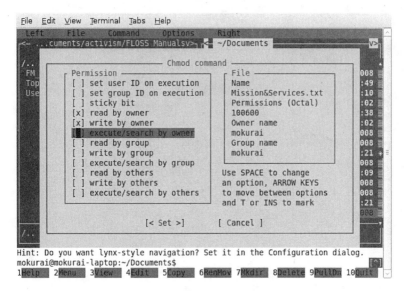

The Commander provides hints, as in the screenshot above, to alert you to useful functions that you might not discover on your own. This one is particularly useful. Setting this configuration option lets you use the left and right arrow keys to navigate between directories, in the same way that Lynx lets you navigate URLs. There are a great many more configuration options available.

You can set and access bookmarks on a Directory Hotlist within your file system using the **Ctrl +** \ key combination, or by selecting the list on the Commands menu. The dialog lets you create and navigate between named bookmark lists.

There is a great deal more to Midnight Commander, of course. You can learn about other functions in the Help dialog (**F1**).

EMACS, VI, NANO, PICO

There is a wide choice of text editors to serve a variety of needs. One of the most venerable is Emacs (originally Editing Macros; jocularly Escape, Meta, Alt, Control, Shift, for its profusion of keyboard commands), written in LISP, with the ability to add commands in LISP, and to change any key bindings for commands. It includes the ability to run external commands, including mail and news (Usenet) readers and compilers, so some users do everything from emacs. Some prefer vi (visual editor), which has a similar ability to add commands and change key bindings, but does not replace the command line for its users. Others still, including most of those who do not program for a living, prefer simpler editors such as nano and pico.

In each case, one can invoke an editor and have it load up a file ready to edit in the form

```
$ editor filename
```

Consult specific program documentation for other command-line options and for editing commands and the rest. For example,

http://www.gnu.org/software/emacs/

http://www.ccsf.edu/Pub/Fac/vi.html

http://www.nano-editor.org/

http://www.itd.umich.edu/itcsdocs/r1168/

PR

This adds titles and page numbers to your text files.

```
$ pr /etc/sendmail.cf | less
```

Keep pressing enter to watch the file go past slowly. You can also use **Page Up** and **Page Down** keys, and arrow keys.

LPR

prints a file. Useful for plain text, and can print some other formats (notably PostScript and PDF) if the system has printer drivers that understand those formats.

```
$ lpr .profile
```

SPLIT

Suppose you have a 600MB ISO file you'd like to split into several pieces for easier storage. You can do so with:

```
$ split -b 200m image.iso image_iso_
```

This example generates three files named *image.iso_aa*, *image.iso_ab*, and *image.iso_ac*, each 200MB in size. If you want to join them again, use the command:

```
$ cat image.iso_* > new-image.iso
```

Remember, the more you practice, the easier and more efficient you can work. Experiment with these commands --the only way to get better at using them is practice!

44. OUTLINE

Feel free to improvise over this outline by adding new sections, chapters etc

This book is an introduction to using the shell with a focus on empowering GNU/Linux newbies. This page has an outline. The book itself is being written at:

http://en.flossmanuals.net/bin/view/CommandLineIntro/WebHome

It is meant to be fun and encourage the reader to play, so it is not organized in a formal manner (for instance, discussing all metacharacters in one place). Instead, features are introduced in the context of useful tasks. Rarely used features are not discussed.

The main topic is the GNU/Linux Bash shell, but useful features of the Korn shell and zsh may be introduced in advanced chapters. The C family of shells and non-Unix shells are beyond the scope of the book.

It assumes the reader is familiar with graphical interfaces, and refers to one or more free desktop environments where discussions of GUIs are necessary.

1. Put yourself in command: why knowing the command line is useful
   1. Example: show a set of operations that require many menus and clicks to accomplish in a GUI (for instance, image manipulation) and then how to do the same things in a single command (for instance, using ImageMagick).
   2. The value of scripting
   3. Other places where command-line skills are useful
      1. Working over a network (when remote terminals or X redirection are unavailable or too slow)
      2. At jobs and cron jobs
      3. Invoking commands through GUI launchers
      4. Seeing what's going on (ps output, other system trouble-shooting)
1. Getting started
   1. What do we mean by a "command"?
   2. What ways can you enter commands?
      1. Opening a terminal window
      2. Alternative ways to run a command on various popular desktops
   3. Different shells
      1. This book focuses on Bash
      2. We tell you what's non-portable (doesn't work with older shells)

4. Privileged (superuser) commands
1. sudo
2. su
1. Beginning syntax: command-line options
1. Moving around directories

      1.   Pathnames

           1.   simple, absolute, and relative

      2.   The . and .. directories

      3.   cd, pushd, etc.

2. Pathnames (syntax)
3. Using the history (through the readline facility)
   1. Emacs mode
   2. vi mode
4. A few useful bits of syntax
1. Enclosing strings in quotation marks
2. Escaping special characters through quotation marks and backslashes
3. Continuing a command over multiple lines
4. White space as separators (any amount is treated the same)
1. Basic commands
1. Commands people use every day
1. pwd
2. ls -al
3. cd
4. chown
5. chmod
6. more, less
7. mv
8. cp
9. rm
10. wc
11. diff
12. gzip, gunzip, gzcat
13. rm, rmdir
14. mkdir
15. find
16. grep
17. passwd
18. kill
19. telnet, ssh
20. ftp

21. apt-get, yum
22. echo
23. setenv, unset
24. du -h
25. lynx
26. ln
1. Permissions
    1. Viewing through ls
    2. Setting through chmod
        1. +x syntax
        2. 777 octal syntax (a figure is useful to show bits
2. Manipulating processes
    1. Interrupting (CTRL-C)
    2. ps and kill
    3. Processes and jobs (background)
3. Redirection
    1. Using < and > and variations
    2. File descriptors (standard input, output, and error)
1. Cheaper by the dozen: operating on lots of files in a single command
1. Globbing
2. The find command
3. The "for" control construct
1. All that typing is too much work
    1. Command and filename completion
    2. Using the history, part 2 (through the ! and ^ facilities)
    3. Aliases
    4. Functions
1. More command-line mastery
    1. Piping commands
    2. Taking advantage of the exit status
        1. The if/then construct
        2. The && and || constructs
    3. Subcommands
        1. The $(command) syntax
        2. The `` backtick syntax
    4. Parameter substitution
    5. Multiple and remote sessions
        1. GNU Screen
        2. SSH
        3. Virtual terminals (GNU/Linux)
2. Useful customizations
    1. Variables
        1. Syntax
        2. Environment variables

45. LICENSE

All chapters copyright of the authors (see below). Unless otherwise stated all chapters in this manual licensed with the **Free Documentation License.**

This documentation is free documentation; you can redistribute it and/or modify it under the terms of the GNU Free Documentation License as published by the Free Software Foundation; either version 1.3 of the License, or (at your option) any later version.

This documentation is distributed in the hope that it will be useful, but WITHOUT ANY WARRANTY; without even the implied warranty of MERCHANTABILITY or FITNESS FOR A PARTICULAR PURPOSE. See the GNU Free Documentation License for more details.

You should have received a copy of the GNU Free Documentation License along with this documentation; if not, write to the Free Software Foundation, Inc., 51 Franklin Street, Fifth Floor, Boston, MA 02110-1301, USA.

46. AUTHORS

Some material taken from the great manual by Gareth Anderson :

http://tldp.org/LDP/GNU-Linux-Tools-Summary/html/

and from :

http://www.gnu.org/software/bash/manual/bashref.html

ABOUT THIS MANUAL
© Free Software Foundation 2009
Modifications:
adam hyde 2009
Peter Brown 2009
Scott Walck 2009
Tom Boyle 2009
Viktor Becher 2009

AWK
© Viktor Becher 2009
Modifications:
adam hyde 2009
Andy Oram 2009
Edward Cherlin 2009
Freaky Clown 2009
Tom Boyle 2009
Vitor Baptista 2009

BASIC COMMANDS
© Free Software Foundation 2009
Modifications:
adam hyde 2009
Andy Oram 2009
Ben Woodacre 2009
Dennis Kibbe 2009
edoardo batini 2009

Freaky Clown 2009
Marc Mengel 2009
Marcelo Magallon 2009
Max Newell 2009
Peter Davies 2009
Sameer Thahir 2009
Steffen Schaumburg 2009
Tom Boyle 2009

BEGINNING SYNTAX
© Free Software Foundation 2009
Modifications:
adam hyde 2009
Andy Oram 2009
Ben Weissmann 2009
Colin Williams 2009
Edward Cherlin 2009
Jason Woof 2009
Johannes Becher 2009
Leif Biberg Kristensen 2009
Marc Mengel 2009
Marcelo Magallon 2009
Peter Davies 2009
Tom Boyle 2009
Viktor Becher 2009
William Merriam 2009

CHECKING EXIT
© Free Software Foundation 2009
Modifications:
adam hyde 2009
Andy Oram 2009
Edward Cherlin 2009
Jason Woof 2009
Tim Goh 2009
Tom Boyle 2009

COMMAND HISTORY
© Gareth Anderson 2009
Modifications:
adam hyde 2009
Andy Oram 2009

Edward Cherlin 2009
Federico Lucifredi 2009
Freaky Clown 2009
hari raj k 2009
Steffen Schaumburg 2009
Tim Goh 2009
Tom Boyle 2009

INTERACTIVE EDITING
© Viktor Becher 2009
Modifications:
adam hyde 2009
Andy Oram 2009
Dennis Kibbe 2009
Tom Boyle 2009

COMMAND QUICKIE
© Free Software Foundation 2009
Modifications:
adam hyde 2009
Andy Oram 2009
Edward Cherlin 2009
Freaky Clown 2009
John Sullivan 2009
S. Lockwood-Childs 2009
Tom Boyle 2009

CREDITS
© adam hyde 2006, 2007, 2009

CUSTOMISATION
© Steve Revilak 2009
Modifications:
adam hyde 2009
Andy Oram 2009
Edward Cherlin 2009
Freaky Clown 2009
John Sullivan 2009
Tom Boyle 2009
Vitor Baptista 2009

Modifications:
adam hyde 2009
Andy Oram 2009
Darren Hall 2009
Edward Cherlin 2009
Freaky Clown 2009
Ntino Krampis 2009
S. Lockwood-Childs 2009
Tom Boyle 2009

GEDIT
© Free Software Foundation 2009
Modifications:
adam hyde 2009
Edward Cherlin 2009
John Sullivan 2009
Tom Boyle 2009

GETTING STARTED
© Free Software Foundation 2009
Modifications:
adam hyde 2009
Andy Oram 2009
Barbaros Catkan 2009
Edward Cherlin 2009
Freaky Clown 2009
John Sullivan 2009
Matt Lee 2009
S. Lockwood-Childs 2009
Tom Boyle 2009
Viktor Becher 2009

GLOSSARY
© Dave Pawson 2009
Modifications:
adam hyde 2009
Edward Cherlin 2009
Freaky Clown 2009
John Sullivan 2009
Michel Barakat 2009
Tom Boyle 2009
Vitor Baptista 2009

INSTALLING SOFTWARE
© Free Software Foundation 2009
Modifications:
adam hyde 2009
Andy Oram 2009
Edward Cherlin 2009
Jarkko Oranen 2009
John Sullivan 2009
Tom Boyle 2009

INTRODUCTION
© Free Software Foundation 2006
Modifications:
adam hyde 2006, 2007, 2009
Andy Oram 2009
Ben Weissmann 2009
Freaky Clown 2009
Michel Barakat 2009
Peter Davies 2009
S. Lockwood-Childs 2009
Scott Walck 2009
Tom Boyle 2009
Viktor Becher 2009
William Merriam 2009

KEDIT
© Free Software Foundation 2009
Modifications:
adam hyde 2009
Edward Cherlin 2009
Matt Lee 2009
Tom Boyle 2009
Vance Kochenderfer 2009

MAINTAINING SCRIPTS
© Free Software Foundation 2009
Modifications:
adam hyde 2009
Andy Oram 2009
Edward Cherlin 2009
Freaky Clown 2009

Marcelo Magallon 2009
Michael Gauland 2009
Tom Boyle 2009
Vitor Baptista 2009

MOVING AROUND
© Free Software Founation 2009
Modifications:
adam hyde 2009
Andy Oram 2009
Edward Cherlin 2009
Freaky Clown 2009
Peter Davies 2009
Steffen Schaumburg 2009
Tom Boyle 2009

MULTIPLE FILES
© Free Software Foundation 2009
Modifications:
adam hyde 2009
Andy Oram 2009
Darren Hall 2009
Edward Cherlin 2009
hari raj k 2009
Kent Tenney 2009
Marcelo Magallon 2009
Peter Davies 2009
Steffen Schaumburg 2009
Tom Boyle 2009

NANO
© Free Software Foundation 2009
Modifications:
adam hyde 2009
Andy Oram 2009
Edward Cherlin 2009
Scott Wells 2009
Tom Boyle 2009

OTHER LANGUAGES
© Andy Oram 2009
Modifications:

PIPING
© Free Software Foundation 2009
Modifications:
adam hyde 2009
Andy Oram 2009
Edward Cherlin 2009
Leif Biberg Kristensen 2009
Tom Boyle 2009
Vance Kochenderfer 2009

PROCESSES
© Free Software Foundation 2009
Modifications:
Edward Cherlin 2009
Tom Boyle 2009

PYTHON
© Free Software Foundation 2009
Modifications:
adam hyde 2009
Freaky Clown 2009
Scott Walck 2009
Tom Boyle 2009

REDIRECTION
© Free Software Foundation 2009
Modifications:
Edward Cherlin 2009
Tom Boyle 2009

REGULAR EXPRESSIONS
© Andy Oram 2009
Modifications:
adam hyde 2009
Darren Hall 2009
Edward Cherlin 2009
Freaky Clown 2009
Tom Boyle 2009

RUBY
© Free Software Foundation 2009

Modifications:
adam hyde 2009
Ben Weissmann 2009
Edward Cherlin 2009
Freaky Clown 2009
Tom Boyle 2009
Vitor Baptista 2009
Xie Haichao 2009

SED
© Freaky Clown 2009
Modifications:
adam hyde 2009
Andy Oram 2009
Darren Hall 2009
Edward Cherlin 2009
Tom Boyle 2009

SSH
© Free Software Foundation 2009
Modifications:
adam hyde 2009
Andy Oram 2009
Freaky Clown 2009
Scott Walck 2009
Tom Boyle 2009

SCRIPTING
© Free Software Foundation 2009
Modifications:
adam hyde 2009
Andy Oram 2009
Beth Skwarecki 2009
edoardo batini 2009
Max Newell 2009
Tom Boyle 2009

SEARCHING FOR FILES
© Free Software Foundation 2009
Modifications:
Tom Boyle 2009

STANDARD FILES
© Free Software Foundation 2009
Modifications:
adam hyde 2009
Andy Oram 2009
Dev Devarajan 2009
Edward Cherlin 2009
Freaky Clown 2009
Marc Mengel 2009
Michael Gauland 2009
Michel Barakat 2009
Tom Boyle 2009
Viktor Becher 2009
Vitor Baptista 2009

SUB COMMANDS
© Free Software Foundation 2009
Modifications:
adam hyde 2009
Andy Oram 2009
Edward Cherlin 2009
Freaky Clown 2009
John Sullivan 2009
Tom Boyle 2009

SUPERUSERS
© Andy Oram 2009
Modifications:
adam hyde 2009
Edward Cherlin 2009
John Sullivan 2009
Tom Boyle 2009

TEXT EDITORS
© Free Software Foundation 2009
Modifications:
adam hyde 2009
Andy Oram 2009
Edward Cherlin 2009
John Sullivan 2009
mike mcneely 2009
Renato Golin 2009

Tom Boyle 2009

Free manuals for free software

COMMAND LINE

GNU Free Documentation License
Version 1.3, 3 November 2008

Copyright (C) 2000, 2001, 2002, 2007, 2008 Free Software Foundation, Inc.
    <http://fsf.org/>
Everyone is permitted to copy and distribute verbatim copies
of this license document, but changing it is not allowed.

0. PREAMBLE

The purpose of this License is to make a manual, textbook, or other
functional and useful document "free" in the sense of freedom: to
assure everyone the effective freedom to copy and redistribute it,
with or without modifying it, either commercially or noncommercially.
Secondarily, this License preserves for the author and publisher a way
to get credit for their work, while not being considered responsible
for modifications made by others.

This License is a kind of "copyleft", which means that derivative
works of the document must themselves be free in the same sense. It
complements the GNU General Public License, which is a copyleft
license designed for free software.

We have designed this License in order to use it for manuals for free
software, because free software needs free documentation: a free
program should come with manuals providing the same freedoms that the
software does. But this License is not limited to software manuals;
it can be used for any textual work, regardless of subject matter or
whether it is published as a printed book. We recommend this License
principally for works whose purpose is instruction or reference.

1. APPLICABILITY AND DEFINITIONS

This License applies to any manual or other work, in any medium, that
contains a notice placed by the copyright holder saying it can be
distributed under the terms of this License. Such a notice grants a
world-wide, royalty-free license, unlimited in duration, to use that
work under the conditions stated herein. The "Document", below,
refers to any such manual or work. Any member of the public is a
licensee, and is addressed as "you". You accept the license if you
copy, modify or distribute the work in a way requiring permission
under copyright law.

A "Modified Version" of the Document means any work containing the Document or a portion of it, either copied verbatim, or with modifications and/or translated into another language.

A "Secondary Section" is a named appendix or a front-matter section of the Document that deals exclusively with the relationship of the publishers or authors of the Document to the Document's overall subject (or to related matters) and contains nothing that could fall directly within that overall subject. (Thus, if the Document is in part a textbook of mathematics, a Secondary Section may not explain any mathematics.) The relationship could be a matter of historical connection with the subject or with related matters, or of legal, commercial, philosophical, ethical or political position regarding them.

The "Invariant Sections" are certain Secondary Sections whose titles are designated, as being those of Invariant Sections, in the notice that says that the Document is released under this License. If a section does not fit the above definition of Secondary then it is not allowed to be designated as Invariant. The Document may contain zero Invariant Sections. If the Document does not identify any Invariant Sections then there are none.

The "Cover Texts" are certain short passages of text that are listed, as Front-Cover Texts or Back-Cover Texts, in the notice that says that the Document is released under this License. A Front-Cover Text may be at most 5 words, and a Back-Cover Text may be at most 25 words.

A "Transparent" copy of the Document means a machine-readable copy, represented in a format whose specification is available to the general public, that is suitable for revising the document straightforwardly with generic text editors or (for images composed of pixels) generic paint programs or (for drawings) some widely available drawing editor, and that is suitable for input to text formatters or for automatic translation to a variety of formats suitable for input to text formatters. A copy made in an otherwise Transparent file format whose markup, or absence of markup, has been arranged to thwart or discourage subsequent modification by readers is not Transparent. An image format is not Transparent if used for any substantial amount of text. A copy that is not "Transparent" is called "Opaque".

Examples of suitable formats for Transparent copies include plain ASCII without markup, Texinfo input format, LaTeX input format, SGML or XML using a publicly available DTD, and standard-conforming simple HTML, PostScript or PDF designed for human modification. Examples of transparent image formats include PNG, XCF and JPG. Opaque formats include proprietary formats that can be read and edited only by proprietary word processors, SGML or XML for which the DTD and/or processing tools are not generally available, and the machine-generated HTML, PostScript or PDF produced by some word processors for output purposes only.

The "Title Page" means, for a printed book, the title page itself, plus such following pages as are needed to hold, legibly, the material this License requires to appear in the title page. For works in formats which do not have any title page as such, "Title Page" means the text near the most prominent appearance of the work's title, preceding the beginning of the body of the text.

The "publisher" means any person or entity that distributes copies of the Document to the public.

A section "Entitled XYZ" means a named subunit of the Document whose title either is precisely XYZ or contains XYZ in parentheses following text that translates XYZ in another language. (Here XYZ stands for a specific section name mentioned below, such as "Acknowledgements", "Dedications", "Endorsements", or "History".) To "Preserve the Title" of such a section when you modify the Document means that it remains a section "Entitled XYZ" according to this definition.

The Document may include Warranty Disclaimers next to the notice which states that this License applies to the Document. These Warranty Disclaimers are considered to be included by reference in this License, but only as regards disclaiming warranties: any other implication that these Warranty Disclaimers may have is void and has no effect on the meaning of this License.

2. VERBATIM COPYING

You may copy and distribute the Document in any medium, either commercially or noncommercially, provided that this License, the copyright notices, and the license notice saying this License applies to the Document are reproduced in all copies, and that you add no other conditions whatsoever to those of this License. You may not use technical measures to obstruct or control the reading or further copying of the copies you make or distribute. However, you may accept compensation in exchange for copies. If you distribute a large enough number of copies you must also follow the conditions in section 3.

You may also lend copies, under the same conditions stated above, and you may publicly display copies.

3. COPYING IN QUANTITY

If you publish printed copies (or copies in media that commonly have printed covers) of the Document, numbering more than 100, and the Document's license notice requires Cover Texts, you must enclose the copies in covers that carry, clearly and legibly, all these Cover Texts: Front-Cover Texts on the front cover, and Back-Cover Texts on the back cover. Both covers must also clearly and legibly identify you as the publisher of these copies. The front cover must present the full title with all words of the title equally prominent and visible. You may add other material on the covers in addition. Copying with changes limited to the covers, as long as they preserve the title of the Document and satisfy these conditions, can be treated as verbatim copying in other respects.

If the required texts for either cover are too voluminous to fit legibly, you should put the first ones listed (as many as fit reasonably) on the actual cover, and continue the rest onto adjacent pages.

If you publish or distribute Opaque copies of the Document numbering more than 100, you must either include a machine-readable Transparent copy along with each Opaque copy, or state in or with each Opaque copy a computer-network location from which the general network-using public has access to download using public-standard network protocols a complete Transparent copy of the Document, free of added material. If you use the latter option, you must take reasonably prudent steps, when you begin distribution of Opaque copies in quantity, to ensure that this Transparent copy will remain thus accessible at the stated location until at least one year after the last time you distribute an Opaque copy (directly or through your agents or retailers) of that edition to the public.

It is requested, but not required, that you contact the authors of the Document well before redistributing any large number of copies, to give them a chance to provide you with an updated version of the Document.

4. MODIFICATIONS

You may copy and distribute a Modified Version of the Document under
the conditions of sections 2 and 3 above, provided that you release
the Modified Version under precisely this License, with the Modified
Version filling the role of the Document, thus licensing distribution
and modification of the Modified Version to whoever possesses a copy
of it. In addition, you must do these things in the Modified Version:

A. Use in the Title Page (and on the covers, if any) a title distinct
   from that of the Document, and from those of previous versions
   (which should, if there were any, be listed in the History section
   of the Document). You may use the same title as a previous version
   if the original publisher of that version gives permission.
B. List on the Title Page, as authors, one or more persons or entities
   responsible for authorship of the modifications in the Modified
   Version, together with at least five of the principal authors of the
   Document (all of its principal authors, if it has fewer than five),
   unless they release you from this requirement.
C. State on the Title page the name of the publisher of the
   Modified Version, as the publisher.
D. Preserve all the copyright notices of the Document.
E. Add an appropriate copyright notice for your modifications
   adjacent to the other copyright notices.
F. Include, immediately after the copyright notices, a license notice
   giving the public permission to use the Modified Version under the
   terms of this License, in the form shown in the Addendum below.
G. Preserve in that license notice the full lists of Invariant Sections
   and required Cover Texts given in the Document's license notice.
H. Include an unaltered copy of this License.
I. Preserve the section Entitled "History", Preserve its Title, and add
   to it an item stating at least the title, year, new authors, and
   publisher of the Modified Version as given on the Title Page. If
   there is no section Entitled "History" in the Document, create one
   stating the title, year, authors, and publisher of the Document as
   given on its Title Page, then add an item describing the Modified
   Version as stated in the previous sentence.
J. Preserve the network location, if any, given in the Document for
   public access to a Transparent copy of the Document, and likewise
   the network locations given in the Document for previous versions
   it was based on. These may be placed in the "History" section.
   You may omit a network location for a work that was published at
   least four years before the Document itself, or if the original

publisher of the version it refers to gives permission.

K. For any section Entitled "Acknowledgements" or "Dedications",
   Preserve the Title of the section, and preserve in the section all
   the substance and tone of each of the contributor acknowledgements
   and/or dedications given therein.
L. Preserve all the Invariant Sections of the Document,
   unaltered in their text and in their titles. Section numbers
   or the equivalent are not considered part of the section titles.
M. Delete any section Entitled "Endorsements". Such a section
   may not be included in the Modified Version.
N. Do not retitle any existing section to be Entitled "Endorsements"
   or to conflict in title with any Invariant Section.
O. Preserve any Warranty Disclaimers.

If the Modified Version includes new front-matter sections or
appendices that qualify as Secondary Sections and contain no material
copied from the Document, you may at your option designate some or all
of these sections as invariant. To do this, add their titles to the
list of Invariant Sections in the Modified Version's license notice.
These titles must be distinct from any other section titles.

You may add a section Entitled "Endorsements", provided it contains
nothing but endorsements of your Modified Version by various
parties--for example, statements of peer review or that the text has
been approved by an organization as the authoritative definition of a
standard.

You may add a passage of up to five words as a Front-Cover Text, and a
passage of up to 25 words as a Back-Cover Text, to the end of the list
of Cover Texts in the Modified Version. Only one passage of
Front-Cover Text and one of Back-Cover Text may be added by (or
through arrangements made by) any one entity. If the Document already
includes a cover text for the same cover, previously added by you or
by arrangement made by the same entity you are acting on behalf of,
you may not add another; but you may replace the old one, on explicit
permission from the previous publisher that added the old one.

The author(s) and publisher(s) of the Document do not by this License
give permission to use their names for publicity for or to assert or
imply endorsement of any Modified Version.

5. COMBINING DOCUMENTS

You may combine the Document with other documents released under this License, under the terms defined in section 4 above for modified versions, provided that you include in the combination all of the Invariant Sections of all of the original documents, unmodified, and list them all as Invariant Sections of your combined work in its license notice, and that you preserve all their Warranty Disclaimers.

The combined work need only contain one copy of this License, and multiple identical Invariant Sections may be replaced with a single copy. If there are multiple Invariant Sections with the same name but different contents, make the title of each such section unique by adding at the end of it, in parentheses, the name of the original author or publisher of that section if known, or else a unique number. Make the same adjustment to the section titles in the list of Invariant Sections in the license notice of the combined work.

In the combination, you must combine any sections Entitled "History" in the various original documents, forming one section Entitled "History"; likewise combine any sections Entitled "Acknowledgements", and any sections Entitled "Dedications". You must delete all sections Entitled "Endorsements".

6. COLLECTIONS OF DOCUMENTS

You may make a collection consisting of the Document and other documents released under this License, and replace the individual copies of this License in the various documents with a single copy that is included in the collection, provided that you follow the rules of this License for verbatim copying of each of the documents in all other respects.

You may extract a single document from such a collection, and distribute it individually under this License, provided you insert a copy of this License into the extracted document, and follow this License in all other respects regarding verbatim copying of that document.

7. AGGREGATION WITH INDEPENDENT WORKS

A compilation of the Document or its derivatives with other separate and independent documents or works, in or on a volume of a storage or distribution medium, is called an "aggregate" if the copyright

resulting from the compilation is not used to limit the legal rights
of the compilation's users beyond what the individual works permit.
When the Document is included in an aggregate, this License does not
apply to the other works in the aggregate which are not themselves
derivative works of the Document.

If the Cover Text requirement of section 3 is applicable to these
copies of the Document, then if the Document is less than one half of
the entire aggregate, the Document's Cover Texts may be placed on
covers that bracket the Document within the aggregate, or the
electronic equivalent of covers if the Document is in electronic form.
Otherwise they must appear on printed covers that bracket the whole
aggregate.

8. TRANSLATION

Translation is considered a kind of modification, so you may
distribute translations of the Document under the terms of section 4.
Replacing Invariant Sections with translations requires special
permission from their copyright holders, but you may include
translations of some or all Invariant Sections in addition to the
original versions of these Invariant Sections. You may include a
translation of this License, and all the license notices in the
Document, and any Warranty Disclaimers, provided that you also include
the original English version of this License and the original versions
of those notices and disclaimers. In case of a disagreement between
the translation and the original version of this License or a notice
or disclaimer, the original version will prevail.

If a section in the Document is Entitled "Acknowledgements",
"Dedications", or "History", the requirement (section 4) to Preserve
its Title (section 1) will typically require changing the actual
title.

9. TERMINATION

You may not copy, modify, sublicense, or distribute the Document
except as expressly provided under this License. Any attempt
otherwise to copy, modify, sublicense, or distribute it is void, and
will automatically terminate your rights under this License.

However, if you cease all violation of this License, then your license

from a particular copyright holder is reinstated (a) provisionally,
unless and until the copyright holder explicitly and finally
terminates your license, and (b) permanently, if the copyright holder
fails to notify you of the violation by some reasonable means prior to
60 days after the cessation.

Moreover, your license from a particular copyright holder is
reinstated permanently if the copyright holder notifies you of the
violation by some reasonable means, this is the first time you have
received notice of violation of this License (for any work) from that
copyright holder, and you cure the violation prior to 30 days after
your receipt of the notice.

Termination of your rights under this section does not terminate the
licenses of parties who have received copies or rights from you under
this License. If your rights have been terminated and not permanently
reinstated, receipt of a copy of some or all of the same material does
not give you any rights to use it.

10. FUTURE REVISIONS OF THIS LICENSE

The Free Software Foundation may publish new, revised versions of the
GNU Free Documentation License from time to time. Such new versions
will be similar in spirit to the present version, but may differ in
detail to address new problems or concerns. See
http://www.gnu.org/copyleft/.

Each version of the License is given a distinguishing version number.
If the Document specifies that a particular numbered version of this
License "or any later version" applies to it, you have the option of
following the terms and conditions either of that specified version or
of any later version that has been published (not as a draft) by the
Free Software Foundation. If the Document does not specify a version
number of this License, you may choose any version ever published (not
as a draft) by the Free Software Foundation. If the Document
specifies that a proxy can decide which future versions of this
License can be used, that proxy's public statement of acceptance of a
version permanently authorizes you to choose that version for the
Document.

11. RELICENSING

"Massive Multiauthor Collaboration Site" (or "MMC Site") means any

World Wide Web server that publishes copyrightable works and also
provides prominent facilities for anybody to edit those works. A
public wiki that anybody can edit is an example of such a server. A
"Massive Multiauthor Collaboration" (or "MMC") contained in the site
means any set of copyrightable works thus published on the MMC site.

"CC-BY-SA" means the Creative Commons Attribution-Share Alike 3.0
license published by Creative Commons Corporation, a not-for-profit
corporation with a principal place of business in San Francisco,
California, as well as future copyleft versions of that license
published by that same organization.

"Incorporate" means to publish or republish a Document, in whole or in
part, as part of another Document.

An MMC is "eligible for relicensing" if it is licensed under this
License, and if all works that were first published under this License
somewhere other than this MMC, and subsequently incorporated in whole or
in part into the MMC, (1) had no cover texts or invariant sections, and
(2) were thus incorporated prior to November 1, 2008.

The operator of an MMC Site may republish an MMC contained in the site
under CC-BY-SA on the same site at any time before August 1, 2009,
provided the MMC is eligible for relicensing.

ADDENDUM: How to use this License for your documents

To use this License in a document you have written, include a copy of
the License in the document and put the following copyright and
license notices just after the title page:

    Copyright (c) YEAR YOUR NAME.
    Permission is granted to copy, distribute and/or modify this document
    under the terms of the GNU Free Documentation License, Version 1.3
    or any later version published by the Free Software Foundation;
    with no Invariant Sections, no Front-Cover Texts, and no Back-Cover Texts.
    A copy of the license is included in the section entitled "GNU
    Free Documentation License".

If you have Invariant Sections, Front-Cover Texts and Back-Cover Texts,
replace the "with...Texts." line with this:

    with the Invariant Sections being LIST THEIR TITLES, with the

Front-Cover Texts being LIST, and with the Back-Cover Texts being LIST.

If you have Invariant Sections without Cover Texts, or some other combination of the three, merge those two alternatives to suit the situation.

If your document contains nontrivial examples of program code, we recommend releasing these examples in parallel under your choice of free software license, such as the GNU General Public License, to permit their use in free software.